ENZO ANGELUCCI   PAOLO MATRICARDI

COMBAT AIRCRAFT
OF WORLD WAR II
1938-1939

Illustrations by Pierluigi Pinto

MILITARY PRESS
New York

In this poster book the tables
are designed so that if you want
you can frame them.
For the single ones cut along the dashed line,
whereas the twin tables
can be pulled out of the book
by cutting the binding thread.

This 1987 edition
published by Military Press
distributed by Crown Publishers, Inc.,
225 Park Avenue South,
New York, New York 10003
Hardcover Edition published by Orion Books,

Created by ADRIANO ZANNINO
Editorial assistant SERENELLA GENOESE ZERBI
Editor: Maria Luisa Ficarra
Translated from the Italian by Ruth Taylor

Consultant for color plate Bruno Benvenuti

ISBN 0-517-64177-1

Color separation SEBI s.r.l., Milan
Typesetting Tipocrom s.r.l., Rome

Printed in Italy by SAGDOS S.p.A., Milan

THE FORMULA OF THE MODERN FIGHTER

A monoplane configuration with cantilever wing, all-metal airframe and covering, retractable landing gear and enclosed cockpit, variable pitch propellers; a performance, thanks to engines of no less than 1,000 hp fitted with superchargers, consisting of speeds around 350 mph (560 km/h) and over at an altitude of more than 29,600 ft (9,000 m); armament consisting of 4 to 8 machine guns, integrated by cannons. When the formula of the modern fighter appeared, definitively replacing the biplane, these were its basic characteristics. Although its conception was an integral part of the great development that marked aeronautical technology during the "golden years" of aviation, its introduction and diffusion were relatively slow. In fact, well into the 1930s, most strategists and military high commands considered the biplane fighter to be the best expression of the pure combat plane, despite the fact that, even with the appearance of the first monoplanes, this formula, whose origins were to be found in the experiences of World War I, had undergone very few basic changes.

As always, the imminence of a new conflict constituted the greatest stimulus to aircraft development and, as always, those countries that were most involved in preparing for combat were the ones that led the progress of aircraft technology. Germany and Great Britain were the nations that led this new phase, the former under the impetus of a frenetic rearmament program, the latter in the certainty of having to prepare in time to oppose Hitler's aggression. In fact, the German and British aeronautical industries became the world leaders in the fighter sector, rapidly making up for years of delay. The results of this development were represented by the Messerschmitt Bf.109 and by the Supermarine Spitfire, great and immediate adversaries. Conceived almost contemporaneously and considered the ancestors of all the pure combat planes that were to emerge from the conflict, the evolution of each of the two fighters was, from many points of view, conditioned by the existence of the other, as well as by the fierce and continuous confrontation in the skies of Europe in which they participated, beginning with the Battle of Britain. Their appearance brought the era of the biplane to a final close and imposed new technological and performance standards that would subsequently be adopted by aircraft manufacturers throughout the world.

In terms of time, however, the German aeronautical industry had been in the vanguard since 1934, the year in which Willy Messerschmitt and Walter Rethel had begun to design the Bf.109, managing to transform their creation into an operative fighter almost a year ahead of its rival. In Great Britain, at that time, directions had already been issued for the drawing up of a new plan for the expansion and modernization of the Royal Air Force and a similar project was in its initial stages on the drawing board of Hawker's chief designer, Sydney Camm. However, the aircraft that was to emerge the following year (the Hurricane) could not be considered competitive with the Messerschmitt. In fact, the influences in the project that derived from Camm's previous work were too strong, Camm being the "father" of some of the most famous British biplane fighters of the 1920s, such as the Fury and the Demon. Although it was modern, with excellent armament and good overall performance, the Hurricane was, in fact, a transitional aircraft and it did not possess the intrinsic development potential that characterized the airframe of the Bf.109. As for the Spitfire project, this was still in an initial definition phase.

The prototype of the Messerschmitt fighter appeared in September 1935 (the Hurricane followed on November 6, while the Spitfire took to the air for the first time on March 5 the following year), and reached its first optimal configuration in the 1939 E version. It was a powerful and compact single-seater, with modern structure, carefully studied aerodynamics, and, more particularly, it was completely integrated with one of the most valid power plants ever produced by the German industry, the Daimler Benz "V-12" injection engine, whose evolution was to characterize that of the aircraft that carried it. The great potential of the Bf.109 was widely publicized, not only in combat operations such as those during the Spanish conflict, but also in sporting endeavors that revealed its features to the world. Outstanding among these was the setting of a world speed record of 379.07 mph (610.43 km/h) in November 1937.

Apart from its extensive activity in combat, the Bf.109's role in the German aeronautical arsenal during World War II can be clearly seen from its production figures: from 1936 to 1945, almost 35,000 were built, the highest number for any aircraft in the entire war and almost two-thirds of the total number of single-seater fighters produced by Germany.

In Britain, the "load" carried by the Spitfire was similar, and it was to become the very symbol of the spirit of the nation. No fewer than 20,531 of these aircraft, in approximately 40 versions, came off the production lines between March 1937 and October 1947, a quantity superior to that of any other British aircraft.

However, without a doubt, Reginald J. Mitchell's project proved to be potentially more powerful than Willy Messerschmitt's, and the aircraft's qualities were exploited to the full in a continuous series of improvements that allowed the Spitfire to sustain the front-line of the Royal Air Force brilliantly up to the late 1950s, well into the jet age. In the final versions, the fighter was powered by no less than a 2,375 hp Rolls-Royce Griffon 67 engine (Spitfire F.XVIII) and it reached its maximum performance of 450 mph (725 km/h) in the Spitfire F.22.

Today, historians and technicians are unanimous in maintaining that the Spitfire's great potential was the direct result of the philosophy that lay behind its design. In fact, the origins of this "immortal" of aviation represent perhaps the clearest example of the great influence that sporting events had on the development of the aeronautical industry in the period between the two wars.

Reginald J. Mitchell, the Spitfire's creator, was also "father" to a series of seaplane racers prepared by Great Britain beginning in 1925 in order to participate in the prestigious Schneider Cup speed race. This series culminated in the Supermarine S.6B, which won the coveted trophy definitively on September 13, 1931, flying at an average speed of 339.82 mph (547.22 km/h).

Starting from the first of the series (the S.4 of 1925), via the S.5, which won the 1927 edition of the race held in Venice and the S.6, which won the 1929 edition at the Isle of Wight and right up to the S.6B, Mitchell proceeded with a logical development that he was to propose almost in its entirety in his future fighter. Structural improvements, for example, or aerodynamic ones, or simply technological refinements regarding the engines and their accessories, or the propellers. All this was aimed at obtaining maximum performance, pursuing the aircraft's oldest challenge, speed.

The experience and technological know-how acquired during this work did not serve only Mitchell. He was brilliantly supported in his designs by the enthusiasm of Henry Royce, a prestigious engine manufacturer, who, for the Supermarine S.6 and S.6B, prepared the first examples of his new "V-12" R model, capable of generating no less than 1,900/2,350 hp. This excellent engine was to be the ancestor of the future Merlin, the very same engine that was to constitute the heart of the Spitfire.

1938

December	In Spain, the decisive offensive of Franco begins. Italy and Germany provide a fundamental contribution by sending aircraft units. In practice, the two nations test the best of their aeronautical products in combat. In the German Condor Legion Heinkel He.111 and Dornier Do.17 bombers, as well as Junkers Ju.87 Stuka attack aircraft, are present.

1939

February 27	Great Britain and France recognize Franco's government.
March 15	The Germans occupy Bohemia-Moravia, forming a protectorate and marking the end of the Czechoslovakian Republic.
April 1	The end of the Spanish Civil War. Franco's government is also recognized by the United States.
April 7	Italian troops occupy Albania.
April 28	Hitler denounces the ten-year pact of non-aggression signed in 1934 with Poland.
May 22	Italy and Germany sign the Pact of Steel, a socio-political agreement ratifying the identity of intent between the two countries.
August 23	Germany and the Soviet Union sign a pact of non-aggression in Moscow.
September 1	The German army invades Poland. The attack begins at 4.45 a.m. and, within a few hours, the Polish defense is completely overwhelmed. The Luftwaffe gains supremacy in the air.
September 3	France and Great Britain declare war on Germany.
September 5	The United States declares itself neutral.
September 24	The United States approves the Cash and Carry laws, authorizing, under certain conditions, the sale of military goods to the belligerent countries.
September 27/28	After heroic resistance, Warsaw falls on September 27. Germany and the Soviet Union establish a friendship treaty to decide the partitioning of Poland.
October 6	The Polish campaign is practically concluded.
November 30	The Soviet Union attacks Finland. Helsinki is bombed.

POTEZ 631

Created with the production of a modern heavy fighter in mind, the Potez 63 project eventually gave rise to one of the most prolific and versatile series of combat aircraft to be built by the French aeronautical industry at the time of the conflict. The 63 series, conceived near the end of 1934, generated not only strategic fighters, but also light bombers as well as attack and reconnaissance planes, and by June 1940 a total of more than 1,100 aircraft had been produced. Moreover, this elegant two-engine aircraft remained in active service during the German occupation, and approximately 250 additional planes built in that period served bearing the insignia of the Luftwaffe (which used them for transport and liaison), of the Vichy air force, of the Italian *Regia Aeronautica* (which received 15 aircraft) and of the Rumanian air force.

The project got under way on the basis of precise official specifications issued in October 1934, calling for the construction of an aircraft capable of carrying out three main roles: a two-seater interceptor and escort fighter; a two-seater night fighter; and a three-seater fighter to be used as a controller for directing, via radio, operations carried out by single-seater fighter units. Work began in April of the following year, and the first prototype (the 63.01) took to the air on April 25, 1936, almost a year later. The aircraft was an all-metal low-wing monoplane with retractable landing gear and double rudders. It was powered by a pair of 580 hp Hispano-Suiza 14Hbs radial engines. Following an accident that occurred during landing, which led to the tail fins being redesigned and to the engines being substituted, the prototype was renamed the 630.01 and flight testing resumed on August 3, 1936. In the meantime, a second prototype had been completed, fitted with Gnome-Rhône 14 Mars engines and designated the 631.01. It made its first flight on March 15, 1937. After a series of evaluation tests, production was launched on the basis of an order for 80 Potez 630s and 90 Potez 631s. Delivery to the units began toward the end of 1938, and a total of 207 631s were eventually built.

Meanwhile, the basic project had been amplified, with other variants destined to carry out different roles being produced. The two-seater day bomber, the Potez 633, took to the air at the end of 1937; the first Potez 637, a three-seater reconnaissance plane also used in cooperation with the army, appeared in the summer of 1938; on December 31 of the same year, the prototype of the Potez 63.11, a three-seater tactical reconnaissance plane, took to the air, the last version to go into mass production.

Initially 125 of the Potez 633 version, distinguished by glazing on the front part of the fuselage and by its capacity to transport eight 110 lb (50 kg) bombs internally, were ordered. However, this order was subsequently canceled, although 21 aircraft were exported to Rumania and 10 to Greece, while another 40 were requisitioned by the *Armée de l'Air*. The Potez 637, similar to the 631 but with a glazed central pod for an observer, was considered a transitional model and only 60 were built while awaiting replacement by the more effective Potez 63.11. In this final variant the front and central part of the fuselage and the cockpit were substantially redesigned. By May 31, 1941, 702 of these aircraft had been built, and total production amounted to over 850.

Among the experimental versions that were never followed up, mention should be made of the 635, which derived from the 631 and was intended as a two-seater night bomber armed with two 20 mm cannons installed in the fuselage and pointing upward at a 20 degree angle; the 639, intended for ground attack and featuring a fixed cannon in the belly pointing downward at a 14 degree angle; and the 63.12, which was derived from the 633 and intended for dive-bombing.

color plate
Potez 631 3ème Escadrille Groupe Chasse II/1 Armée de l'Air (3rd Squadron II/1 Fighting Group *Armée de l'Air*) - France 1939

Aircraft:	Potez 631
Nation:	France
Manufacturer:	SNCAN
Type:	Night fighter
Year:	1938
Engine:	2 Gnome-Rhône 14 M6/7, 14-cylinder radial, air-cooled, 660 hp each
Wingspan:	52 ft 8 in (16.00 m)
Length:	36 ft 5 in (11.07 m)
Height:	11 ft 10 in (3.61 m)
Takeoff weight:	9,920 lb (4,500 kg)
Maximum speed:	276 mph (445 km/h) at 13,150 ft (4,000 m)
Ceiling:	29,600 ft (9,000 m)
Range:	760 miles (1,225 km)
Armament:	2 x 20 mm cannons; 8 machine guns
Crew:	2/3

A Potez 63.11 in Syria in 1941. This was one of the aircraft that fought alongside the British, rebelling against the Vichy government.

"The best fighter in the world." In 1937, these words were used at the Brussels Air Show to define the prototype of Morane-Saulnier's latest combat plane, which had recently completed a series of flight tests and official evaluations. Aside from this advertising statement, it became the founder of a long series of over 1,000 aircraft (1,081 to be precise) that were produced up till June 1940 and that earned a prominent place in aviation history for many reasons: the Morane-Saulnier M.S.406 was the first modern aircraft of its category to go into service in the units of the *Armée de l'Air*; it was built in remarkable quantities compared to French production standards of the time, second only to the two-engine Potez 630 series; and, above all, it was the fighter available in the greatest numbers when the war broke out.

The project was launched on the basis of specifications issued in 1934, and the prototype (built in great secrecy) made its first flight on August 8, 1935. Designated the M.S.405, it was a low-wing monoplane with retractable landing gear, powered by an 860 hp Hispano-Suiza 12 Ygrs engine. It had an all-metal airframe with a covering of aluminum, plywood, and canvas, and an enclosed cockpit. The armament consisted of a 20 mm cannon installed in the propeller shaft and two machine guns in the wings.

Right from its first flight, the features of the aircraft proved to be excellent, especially its speed, which reached 303 mph (489 km/h) at 13,200 ft (4,000 m) and just over 250 mph (400 km/h) at sea level. The latter meant that the Morane-Saulnier became the first French fighter to break the 250 mph (400 km/h) barrier. After the initial flight tests, the first prototype was joined by a second (with modifications to the propeller and the wings), and both these aircraft faced a series of official evaluations. At the beginning of 1937, the company received an order for 15 preseries aircraft, and the second of these (which took to the air on May 20, 1938) became the progenitor of the M.S.406: the differences consisted mainly in the use of a different engine, a different type of propeller, and in structural modifications, especially to the wing. The aircraft was chosen for production in this definitive version on the basis of an order that, in March 1938, amounted to 1,000 planes. In order to guarantee this large quantity, assembly lines were set up in several factories and, within a short space of time, the delivery rate was quite high. By September 1939, 572 M.S.406s had already left the factories.

The first unit to receive the new fighter was the 6th *Escadre de Chasse*, in December 1938. Other units followed, and immediately before mobilization in August 1939, 12 groups had been equipped with the aircraft. However, from the beginning of its operational service, it became apparent that the 406 was distinctly inferior to its direct adversary, the Messerschmitt Bf.109E. During the Battle of France, 150 Moranes were lost, as compared to 191 enemy aircraft definitely hit and another 89 probably hit. A further hundred or so Moranes were destroyed on the ground, and about 150 were damaged beyond repair by the French crews to prevent their falling into enemy hands. After the armistice, some Morane 406s remained in service in the Vichy air force (where they were mainly used for training), and others were handed over by the Germans to Finland, which had received 30 aircraft in 1940.

Another foreign buyer was Switzerland, which, after having acquired two M.S.406s, built 82 aircraft on license (designated EFW-3800) as well as 207 of a subsequent home-developed version known as EFW-3801.

Formation of Morane-Saulnier M.S.406s at an airport in Lebanon at the beginning of the war.

An M.S.406, note the cannon in the propeller hub and the retractable radiator.

Aircraft:	Morane-Saulnier M.S.406
Nation:	France
Manufacturer:	SNCAO
Type:	Fighter
Year:	1938
Engine:	Hispano-Suiza 12 Y, 12-cylinder V, liquid-cooled, 860 hp
Wingspan:	34 ft 10 in (10.65 m)
Length:	26 ft 9 in (8.15)
Height:	9 ft 3 in (2.82 m)
Weight:	6,000 lb (2,720 kg) loaded
Maximum speed:	302 mph (486 km/h) at 16,400 ft (5,000 m)
Ceiling:	30,840 ft (9,400 m)
Range:	497 miles (800 km)
Armament:	1 x 20 mm cannon; 2 machine guns
Crew:	1

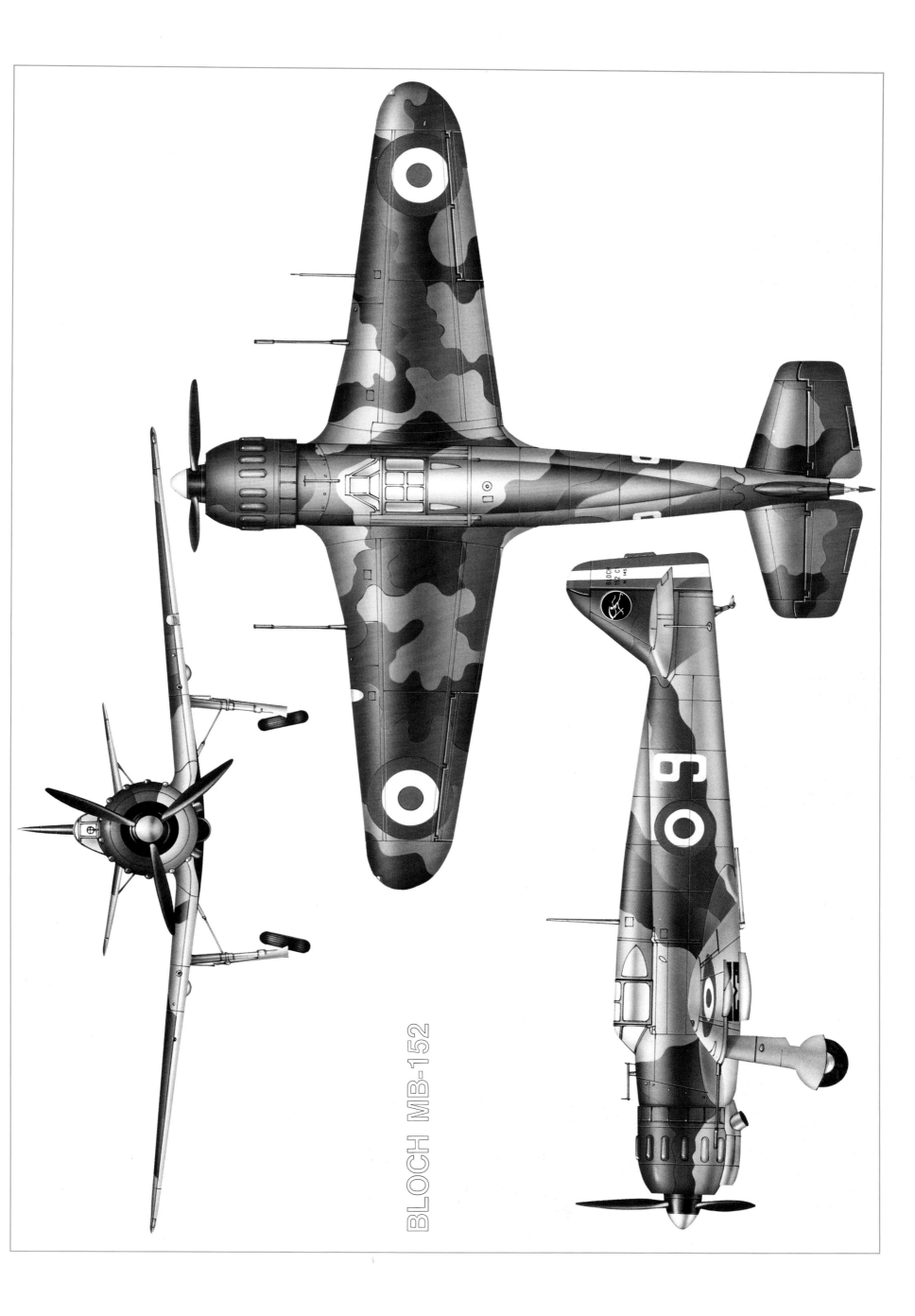

BLOCH MB-152

BLOCH MB-152

The Bloch MB-152 was one of the most widely used French fighters at the time of the German invasion and during the few weeks prior to the armistice. However, this does not mean that it was a particularly competitive aircraft. With the possible exception of the Dewoitine 520, of which very few existed at the time, the *Armée de l'Air*'s front-line fighters were inferior to those of the Luftwaffe. The major limitations of the Bloch MB-152 were its insufficient range, its awkward handling and its obvious inferiority when compared to its direct adversary, the Messerschmitt Bf.109E.

The Bloch MB-152 was the last operational version of a series of aircraft (none of which was really very successful) that originated in 1934 on the basis of official specifications issued by the French military authorities on June 13. The founder of the whole series was the MB-150, the prototype of which appeared on July 17, 1936. The aircraft's complete inadequacy (on its first flight it did not manage takeoff) led to the project initially being laid aside. At the beginning of the following year, however, work on it resumed, and after a series of substantial modifications, the definitive prototype took to the air successfully on September 29, 1937. In April of the following year, after an initial series of evaluations, an order for 25 preseries aircraft was settled, the confirmation of a further order for 450 planes depending on their success.

It was, in fact, preparations for this mass production that threw light on some serious problems that could be solved only by taking radical measures: the Bloch MB-150's structure proved to be unsuitable for the strict demands of mass production, and it therefore became necessary to redesign it completely. In this revised form the aircraft's designation was also changed to MB-151, and the prototype made its maiden flight on August 18, 1938. While maintaining the general configuration of low-wing monoplane with retractable landing gear, powered by a Gnome-Rhône radial engine that drove a three-bladed variable pitch metal propeller, the MB-151 differed from its predecessor in its modified wing profile and in a general redimensioning of the wing itself. During flight testing and evaluation trials, however, the aircraft still proved to be inadequate and, above all, incapable of achieving the performance desired of the project.

In the meantime, the prototype of an improved version had been prepared, designated the MB-152. This fighter, in its turn, differed from its predecessor, especially in its more powerful engine and armament. Its first flight took place at Villacoublay on December 15, 1938, and was followed by an intensive series of flight tests. However, this aircraft also revealed a lack of preparation.

Nevertheless, production went ahead on the basis of a series of orders for both models: 144 MB-151s were commissioned, along with a total of 482 MB-152s. The Bloch fighter went into operational service in the first units of the *Armée de l'Air* in October and November 1939. Following the armistice, the surviving aircraft (51 Bloch MB-151s and 259 Bloch MB-152s) were taken

A Bloch MB-152 with 20 mm cannons mounted in the wings.

over by the Germans, and many of them served in the Vichy air force. Further developments to the project (including the more powerful Bloch MB-155, the prototype of which made its first flight on December 3, 1939, and of which nine were built, as well as the MB-157 model of 1942) came to a virtual halt. Lastly, mention should be made of nine MB-151s that were delivered to Greece beginning in April 1940 as part of an order for 25 aircraft.

---

color plate

Bloch MB-152 Groupe Chasse II/1 Armée de l'Air (II/1 Fighting Group *Armée de l'Air*) - France 1940

Aircraft:	Bloch MB-152
Nation:	France
Manufacturer:	SNCASO
Type:	Fighter
Year:	1939
Engine:	Gnome-Rhône 14 N-25, 14-cylinder radial, air-cooled, 1,080 hp
Wingspan:	34 ft 8 in (10.54 m)
Length:	29 ft 11 in (9.10 m)
Height:	9 ft 11 in (3.03 m)
Takeoff weight:	5,935 lb (2,693 kg)
Maximum speed:	320 mph (515 km/h) at 13,150 ft (4,000 m)
Ceiling:	32,900 ft (10,000 m)
Range:	384 miles (580 km)
Armament:	2 x 20 mm cannons; 2 machine guns
Crew:	1

A Bloch MB-151 during a test flight and still lacking its markings.

FRANCE

On September 3, 1939, when France declared war on Germany, French aviation was still far from reaching a level of overall strength that would have put it on an equal footing with the Luftwaffe. At the time the war broke out, the *Armée de l'Air* had only 1,200 modern combat planes at its disposal, of which 826 were fighters, some not yet operative, and approximately 1,500 aircraft (of which almost 400 were fighters) that dated back to the beginning of the 1930s.

Massive recourse to foreign aircraft had been considered indispensable to make up for the delays in home production and thus to gaine time: the first 100 Curtiss Hawk 75A fighters had been ordered at the end of 1938; in the light-bomber sector, twin-engine Martin 167 Marylands and Douglas DB-7s were requested; as for the heavy-bombers, in December 1939, the French authorities did not hesitate to solicit a hundred or so four-engine B-24s from the United States. Even so, the situation changed very little in the following months, due also to the fact that the headlong rush of events made it impossible for the Allied suppliers to deliver the equipment as planned. By May 10, 1940, the aircraft in front-line service numbered 1,501, 784 fighters.

On the western front the adversary, the Luftwaffe, had more than 3,000 of the most modern aircraft of the period at its disposal. These included 1,000 or so Messerschmitt Bf.109 and Bf.110 fighters; 1,200 Heinkel He.111 bombers; 250 Dornier Do.17 bombers; and 350 Junkers Ju.87 and Ju.88 dive-bombers.

Although the *Armée de l'Air* fought with great honor and sacrifice, faced with such an adversary it was unable to do much, fully paying for the uncertainties and confusion that had characterized its development. The French military aviation, conceived at an organizational level in 1933, officially became the third armed force in the following year, although it did not begin to function as a structure until 1936. It would have had time to become consolidated had its needs been recognized and satisfied in time. This did not occur, for a series of political, strategical and industrial reasons that, in fact, greatly diminished its role and its potential, especially as compared to the modern and efficient German war machine.

Chronology

1938

March 23. The prototype of the Breguet 690, a twin-engine multirole aircraft, takes to the air. It was to go into production in an assault version, designated Breguet 691 AB-2. The aircraft had a limited operative career.

May 20. The definitive prototype of the Morane-Saulnier M.S.406, the most famous French World War II combat plane, takes to the air. The production series based on this aircraft eventually amounted to 1,081 planes. In December, the 6th *Escadre de Chasse* became the first unit to receive the aircraft. Immediately prior to mobilization (August 1939), 12 groups had been reequipped. By September 1939, 572 aircraft had already left the factory.

June. The first production models of the twin-engine Bloch 131 bomber come off the assembly lines. A rather unsatisfactory aircraft, only 121 were built.

September. The prototype of the Caudron C.714, a light fighter, takes to the air. Only a few dozen were to be built.

October 1. The prototype of the Arsenal VG-30, an excellent light-bomber that reached its optimal configuration in the VG-33 model, makes its maiden flight at Villacoublay. At the time of the armistice, 160 of these aircraft were in an advanced stage of construction. During flight testing, the VG-33 reached 365 mph (588 km/h).

October 2. The prototype of the Dewoitine D-520, the best French fighter of the war, makes its maiden flight. Superior in handling to the Messerschmitt Bf.109, 775 of these aircraft were built (out of 2,320 ordered), only 36 of which were operative on May 10, 1940.

December. The Latécoère 298 goes into service. Approximately 200 of this single-engine seaplane bomber were to be built. On May 10, 1940, 50 or so of these planes were in service with 5 ground-based front-line units of the navy.

Initially used for daytime ground attack and for tactical bombing, the Laté 298s proved to be particularly vulnerable compared to the fierce fighters of the Luftwaffe and were subsequently destined for night missions.

December 15. The prototype of the Bloch MB-152 takes to the air at Villacoublay. It was to be one of the most widely used French fighters at the time of the German invasion and in the few weeks that preceded the armistice. It was the last example of a series of aircraft (not particularly outstanding) that originated in 1934, and whose founder was the MB-150 model that appeared as a prototype on July 17, 1936. A total of 482 MB-152s were built. The Bloch fighters went into service in the first units of the *Armée de l'Air* in October/November 1939.

1939

January 5. The prototype of the excellent Bloch 174 twin-engine reconnaissance aircraft makes its maiden flight. Only 50 of these aircraft were to be built.

January 21. The prototype of the Amiot 351, considered one of the most elegant of French combat planes, makes its first flight at Istres. A total of 285 of this series of twin-engine bombers was ordered, although only 47 were operative by the end of May 1940.

March 24. The first production series LeO 451 takes to the air. However, this excellent twin-engine bomber appeared too late: of the 452 aircraft completed at the time of the armistice, only 222 were part of the units on May 10, 1940.

July 10. Maiden flight of the Dewoitine D.720, a twin-engine reconnaissance aircraft of which it was planned to build 1,000. In practice, however, the aircraft proved to be outdated and was not followed up.

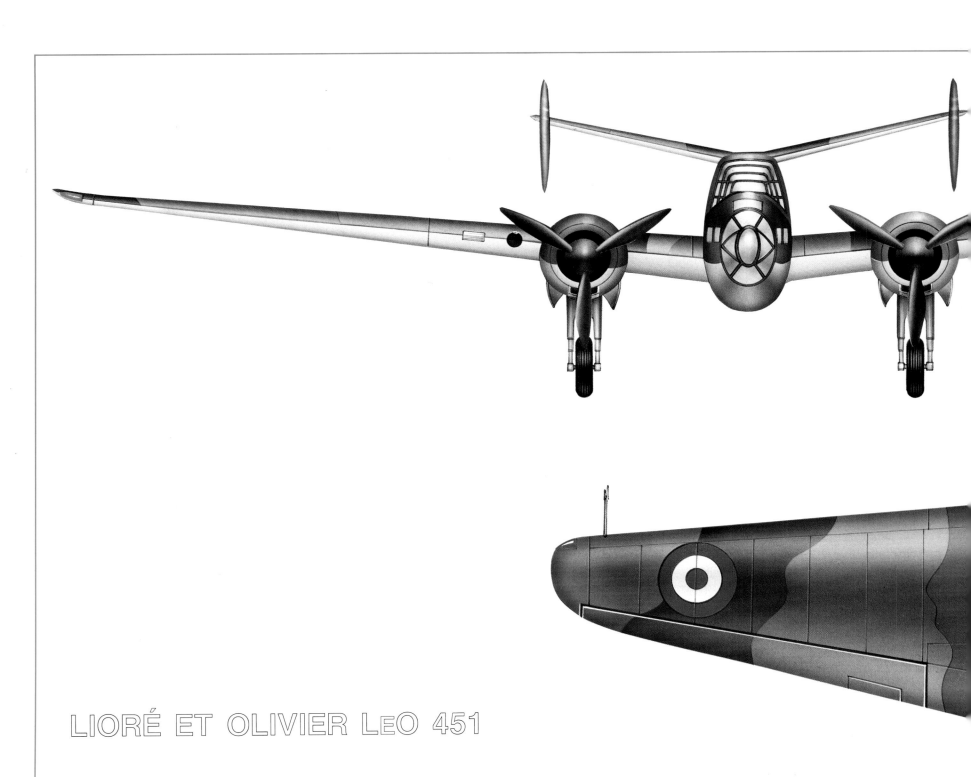

LIORÉ ET OLIVIER LeO 451

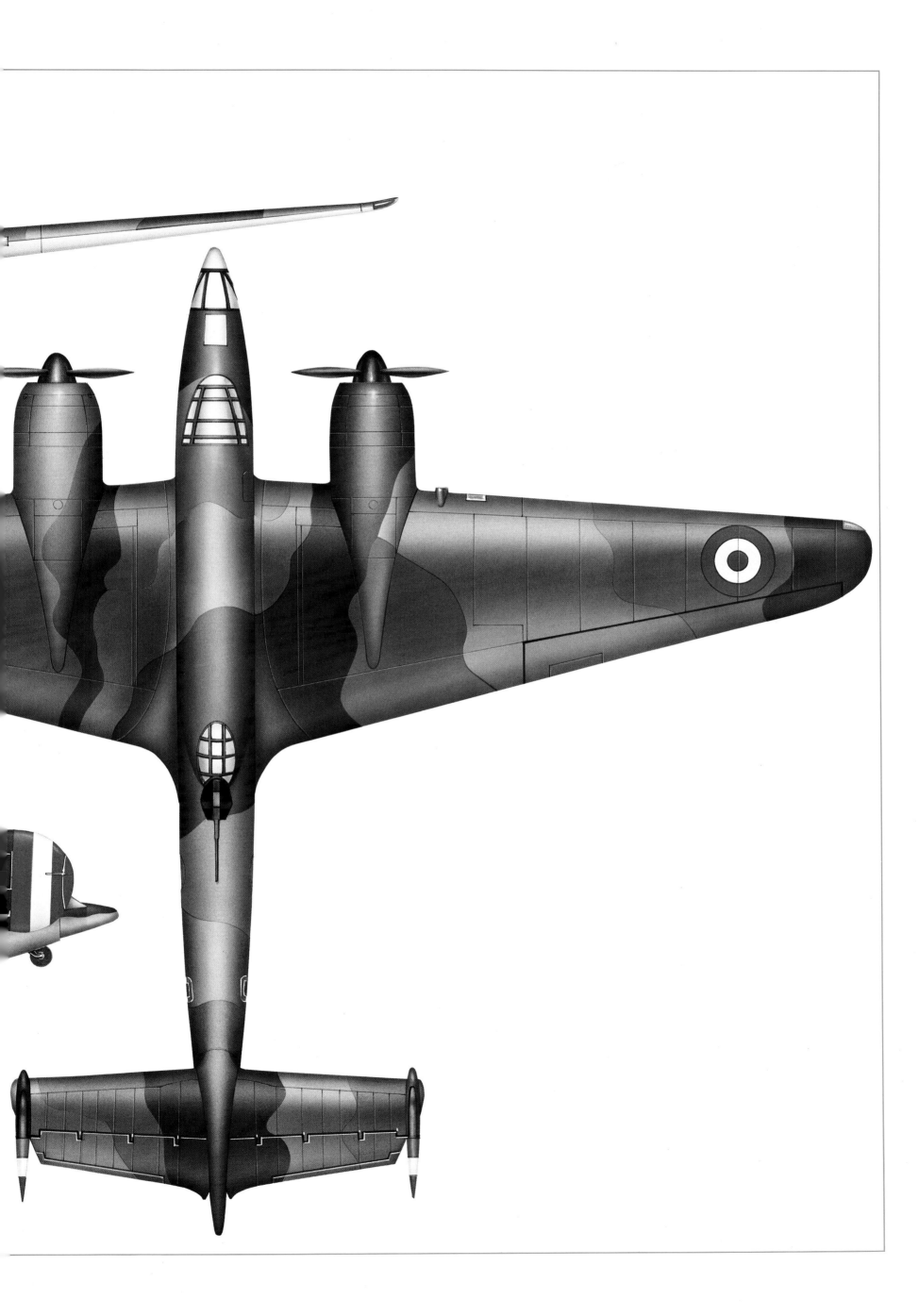

Judged to be one of the best medium bombers in service in the world at the time, the Lioré et Olivier aircraft of the LeO 45 series represented a true evolutionary leap in the *Armée de l'Air*'s equipment. Reasonably advanced in concept, powerful, well armed, and with a performance equal to that of any contemporary fighter, these excellent two-engine aircraft nevertheless appeared too late to make a significant contribution to the course of the war. On May 10, 1940, out of a total of 222 planes forming part of the units, only about half could be considered operational. However, with a total of 452 built up to the time of the armistice and a further 150 built during the German occupation, the LeO 45s served in the Vichy air force and in the navy for the duration of the war, and many of the 67 survivors remained in service after the conflict. The last two LeO 453s (a variant fitted with Pratt & Whitney engines) were not withdrawn until September 1957. From many points of view, this long career can be considered the best recognition of the merits of this bomber, which was the only French aircraft used in the 1939/1940 campaign to remain in active service for no fewer than 12 years after the war ended.

The project originated in response to official specifications issued on November 17, 1937, requesting the aeronautical industry to produce a fast, modern medium bomber to replace the by then obsolete aircraft that constituted the *Armée de l'Air*'s standard equipment. More particularly, the new aircraft was to be capable of carrying up to 3,300 lb (1,500 kg) of bombs at a speed of 250 mph (400 km/h) and have an active range of about 560 miles (900 km). It was to have a four-man crew, and the defensive armament was to include a 20 mm cannon.

Several manufacturers responded to the specifications (including Amiot and Latécoère), but Lioré et Olivier's proposal immediately appeared the most competitive. The prototype (LeO 45-01) made it first flight on January 16, 1937, and apart from some stability problems, its overall performance proved to be excellent. During official evaluations, which commenced on September 2, the aircraft achieved a maximum horizontal speed of 278 mph (480 km/h) at 13,150 ft (4,000 m), while following a dive from 16,500

ft (5,000 m) the aircraft touched 387 mph (624 km/h), demonstrating remarkable qualities of structural strength and streamlining. The LeO 45 was an all-metal low-wing monoplane with retractable landing gear. Its bomb load was completely contained in the fuselage, and the defensive armament consisted of a 20 mm cannon on the aircraft's back, a retractable 7.5 mm machine gun in the belly, and another fixed one in the front of the aircraft.

However, evaluation tests revealed a series of deficiencies in the original engines (Hispano-Suiza 14AA, generating 1,078 hp at takeoff), and when the first contract was drawn up for the production of 20 aircraft in January 1938, a request was made for the installation of equally powerful Gnome-Rhône 14N engines. The prototype was renamed LeO 451-01, and flight testing resumed on October 21, 1938. Meanwhile, orders had been placed for a total of 145 aircraft. The first LeO 451-01 of the series made its maiden flight on March 24, 1939, following schedule delays and by September only five aircraft could be considered operational.

During the occupation, the Germans did not show any particular interest in the bomber. Some were converted for transport, others were assigned to the *Regia Aeronautica*, which incorporated them into the 51st Autonomous Bomber Group. Among the variants in production after the 451, as well as the LeO 453, were the 452, fitted with different Gnome-Rhône engines; the 454, with two Bristol Hercules engines; and, lastly, the 458, with Wright R-2600 engines.

---

color plate

Lioré et Olivier LeO 451 Groupe Reconnaissance II/31 Armée de l'Air (II/31 Reconnaissance Group *Armée de l'Air*) - France 1940

Aircraft:	Lioré et Olivier LeO 451
Nation:	France
Manufacturer:	SNCASE
Type:	Bomber
Year:	1939
Engine:	2 Gnome-Rhône 14N, 14-cylinder radial, air-cooled, 1,140 hp each
Wingspan:	73 ft 10 1/2 in (22.50 m)
Length:	56 ft 4 in (17.17 m)
Height:	17 ft 2 in (5.23 m)
Weight:	25,133 lb (11,385 kg) loaded
Maximum speed:	307 mph (494 km/h) at 15,748 ft (4,800 m)
Ceiling:	29,530 ft (9,000 m)
Range:	1,430 miles (2,300 km)
Armament:	1 x 20 mm cannon; 2 machine guns; 4,400 lb (2,000 kg) of bombs
Crew:	4

The prototype of the LeO 451 with Gnome-Rhône engines.

The prototype of the LeO 451 in its original configuration with Hispano-Suiza engines.

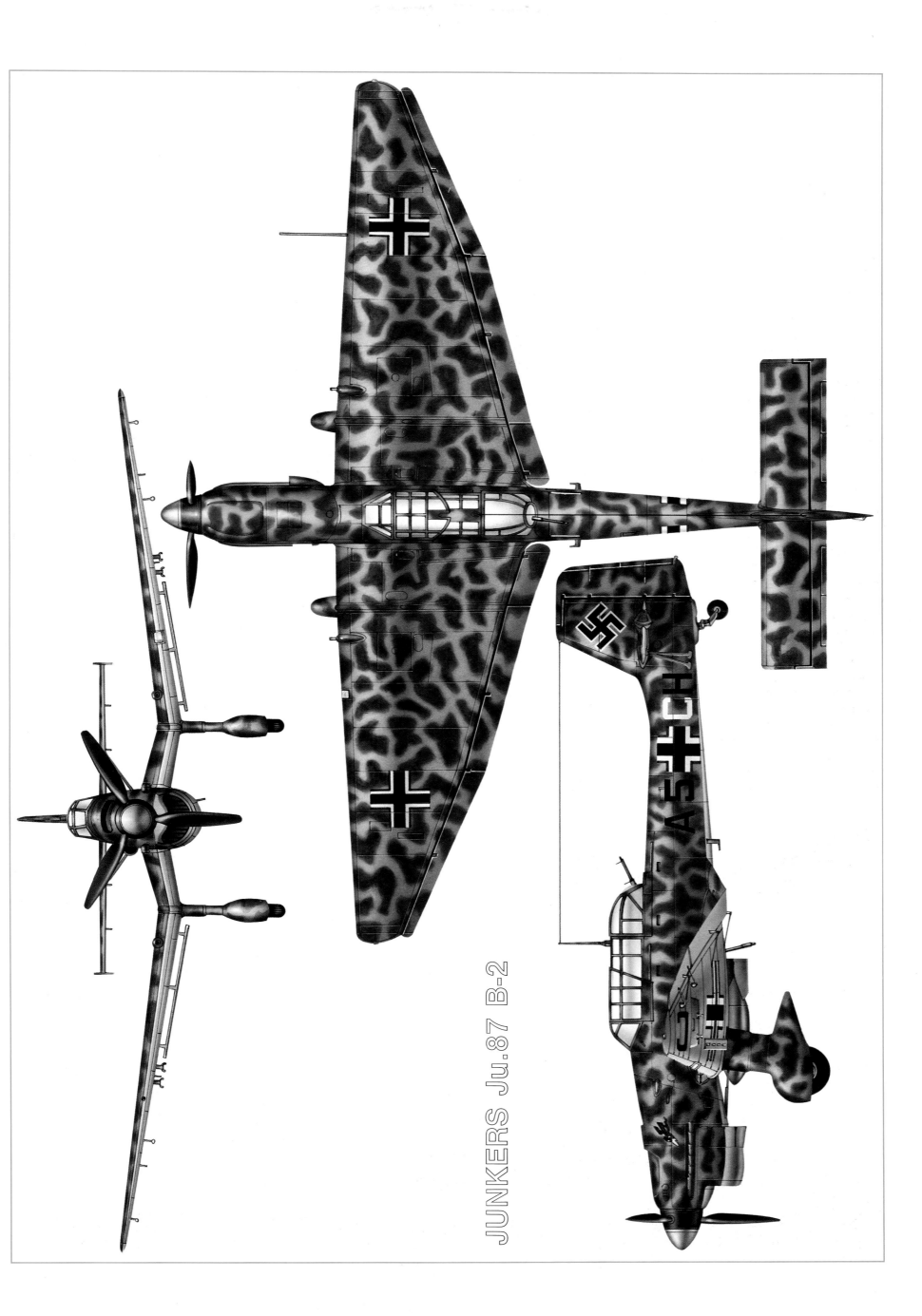

JUNKERS Ju.87 B-2

JUNKERS Ju.87

Designed in 1933, the Junkers Ju.87 Stuka remained in production until 1944. More than 5,700 of these aircraft were completed in a dozen versions, and it went down in history as one of the most widely used combat planes in the entire German aeronautical arsenal. However, apart from this purely quantitative aspect, this ugly and awkward aircraft played a primary role in the gloomy events of World War II, more particularly so because it became (at least in the early years of the conflict) the true symbol of the Luftwaffe's strength. The Stuka (short for *Sturzkampfflugzeug*, the word for dive-bomber used in Germany to indicate all aircraft of this type) was the real protagonist of Germany's lightning war; and it was the Stuka, apart from its actual fighting potential, that sowed terror among its adversaries with the characteristic whistling sound that accompanied its rapid dive toward its target. Even when the myth surrounding this aircraft slowly began the fade (and this commenced during the Battle of Britain), it remained virtually irreplaceable in its role, so much so that the German aeronautical industry proved incapable of producing a substitute of equal value, despite the great progress it made during the war.

The Ju.87 project was launched in 1933, in response to a request from the German military authorities for the construction of an aircraft for use as a dive-bomber. Four manufacturers answered the call (Arado, Blohm und Voss, Heinkel, and Junkers), and in March 1936, after an extensive series of comparative tests, the Junkers prototype was chosen. The aircraft, designed by Hermann Pohlmann, had made its maiden flight at the beginning of 1935, but during the months that followed it had been substantially modified. In fact, the original prototype had been characterized by double tail planes and the use of a British Rolls-Royce Kestrel engine, generating 525 hp at take-off, that drove a two-bladed wooden propeller. The tests brought to light problems in the engines, which had a tendency to overheat, as well as symptoms of structural weakness, and in the second prototype, therefore, a 610 hp Junkers Jumo engine was chosen, and this drove a three-bladed variable pitch metal propeller. More particularly, a single tail plane configuration was adopted. All these modifications, as well as other details, were incorporated into a third prototype, which provided the basis for the first production version.

The Ju.87 had an all-metal airframe and covering, wings of the characteristic "inverted gull" shape, and fixed landing gear housed in large fairings. The main bomb load was installed in a support at the center of the fuselage, while the initial defensive armament consisted of a fixed 7.9 mm machine gun in a half-wing and a similar flexible weapon in the rear of the completely glazed cockpit.

The first production variant (Ju.87 A-1) appeared at the beginning of 1937 and was used mainly as a trainer. Later, these aircraft saw limited combat duty during the Spanish Civil War. In 1938, the initial version was followed by the first variant of the B series (the Ju.87 B-1), characterized by the use of a more powerful Jumo engine and by modifications to the fuselage and empennage. This was the first version to be built in any great number; the second most produced was the D series, in which the aircraft was further improved from a structural and aerodynamic point of view and was provided with more powerful power plants and armament. Deliveries of the first series (Ju.87 D-1) to the units of the Luftwaffe commenced in the spring of 1941; the following year, the final G version was developed from this basic variant and specialized in antitank attack.

color plate
Junkers Ju.87 B-2 Trop. Luftwaffe Gruppe 1/Stukageschwader 1 - North Africa 1941

Aircraft:	Junkers Ju.87 B-1
Nation:	Germany
Manufacturer:	Junkers Flugzeug und Motorenwerke AG
Type:	Attack
Year:	1938
Engine:	Junkers Jumo 211, 12-cylinder V, liquid-cooled, 1,200 hp
Wingspan:	45 ft 3 in (13.79 m)
Length:	36 ft 5 in (11.10 m)
Height:	13 ft 2 in (4.01 m)
Weight:	9,560 lb (4,330 kg) loaded
Maximum speed:	238 mph (383 km/h) at 13,410 ft (4,090 m)
Ceiling:	26,250 ft (8,000 m)
Range:	490 miles (788 km)
Armament:	3 machine guns; 1,100 lb (500 kg) of bombs
Crew:	2

A Ju.87 B belonging to the Stukageschwader 1, damaged and captured by the British in North Africa. Its camouflage is unusual for a German aircraft.

MESSERSCHMITT Bf.109E

From 1936 to 1945, almost 35,000 of these aircraft were built. This figure alone gives an indication of the importance of the Messerschmitt Bf.109 in the German aeronautical arsenal during World War II. However, in the course of its long and extensive career on all fronts, this small, agile, and powerful aircraft acquired a role that went well beyond the purely quantitative dimensions of its production (the highest, without exception, of the entire war), and it fought its way into the ranks of the greatest protagonists of aviation history.

In fact, the appearance of the Bf.109 brought the era of the biplane to a definitive close, imposing qualitative standards that sooner or later were to serve as reference points for aircraft manufacturers throughout the world. From this point of view, Willy Messerschmitt's fighter not only placed Germany suddenly in the vanguard in the field of military aviation, but it also became the progenitor of all the pure combat planes that were to emerge from the conflict. In this latter role, the Bf.109 had a fierce adversary (and not only in the skies over Europe) in another "immortal," the British Supermarine Spitfire, with which it participated in a continuous technological chase, aimed at gaining supremacy in the air and leading to the continuous strengthening and improving of both aircraft.

The Bf.109 originated in the summer of 1934, in response to an official request for a monoplane interceptor with which to replace the Heinkel He.51 and the Arado Ar.68 biplanes. Its designers, Willy Messerschmitt and Walter Rethel, took the excellent features of the four-seater Bf.108 *Taifun* commercial aircraft as their basis and created the smallest possible structure compatible with the most powerful engine then available. The fighter thus took the form of a compact, all-metal, low-wing monoplane with retractable landing gear and an enclosed cockpit. Originally, it had been planned to install the new 610 hp Junkers Jumo 210A engine, but because this power plant was unavailable, the prototype was fitted with a Rolls-Royce Kestrel V engine, generating 695 hp at takeoff and driving a two-bladed wooden propeller.

The aircraft was completed in September 1935, and a month later it began comparative tests together with the other prototypes created in response to the same specifications: the Arado Ar.80, the Heinkel He.112, and the Focke Wulf Fw.159. The final choice left the He.112 and the Bf.109 in the running, and both manufacturers received an order for 10 preseries aircraft. In practice, however, the Messerschmitt project proved to be the best and, in the course of its development, the aircraft was substantially modified, especially in its armament and its engine, which now became the Jumo 210A. The first aircraft of the initial production

Cleaning the armament of a Bf.109E at an airport in the Libyan desert.

series, the Bf.109B, appeared in February 1937, and four months later they were sent to Spain. Experiences in combat removed any remaining doubts concerning the aircraft's remarkable capabilities, and this success was further increased by a series of sporting performances in which, propaganda aside, the Bf.109 was judged the best fighter of the time. In November 1937, a prototype fitted with an engine capable of generating 1,650 hp over short distances broke the world speed record, setting a new one of 379.07 mph (610.43 km/h).

The B variant was followed by the C, with strengthened armament, and then by the D, fitted with Daimler Benz DB 600 engines. This marked the transition toward the first mass-produced version, the Bf.109E, characterized by the use of the more powerful and reliable Daimler Benz DB 601 engine. The first Bf.109E-1s were completed at the beginning of 1939, and total production of the various subseries reached 1,540 within a year. In 1940, 1,868 of these aircraft were built and, with the gradual withdrawal of the previous variants, the fighter assumed the leading role in all the Luftwaffe's operations, especially in the Battle of Britain.

Aircraft:	Messerschmitt Bf.109E-1
Nation:	Germany
Manufacturer:	Messerschmitt AG
Type:	Fighter
Year:	1939
Engine:	Daimler Benz DB 601D, 12-cylinder V, liquid-cooled, 1,050 hp
Wingspan:	32 ft 4 1/2 in (9.87 m)
Length:	28 ft 4 in (8.65 m)
Height:	8 ft 2 in (2.50 m)
Weight:	4,431 lb (2,010 kg) loaded
Maximum speed:	342 mph (550 km/h) at 13,120 ft (4,000 m)
Ceiling:	34,450 ft (10,500 m)
Range:	410 miles (660 km)
Armament:	2 x 20 mm cannons; 2 machine guns
Crew:	1

color plate

Messerschmitt Bf.109E JG.26 Schlageter Kdz. Adolf Galland's plane - France 1940

A Bf.109E returns for dispersal in a Libyan airport.

GERMANY

The Luftwaffe, officially established on March 1, 1935, suddenly revealed itself to be one of the world's most powerful and modern air forces. By the end of the year, its strength amounted to 20,000 men and approximately 1,000 front-line aircraft. The aeronautical industry's production rate was extremely high, 300 aircraft being produced per month.

Sixteen years after the Great War, this achievement represented the high point in a long process of reconstruction of military aviation, as well as the launching of a subsequent phase of expansion that was to continue without interruption throughout World War II.

Throughout the 1920s and early 1930s, the rebirth of the German military air force had been smoldering under the ashes, despite the heavy limitations imposed by the peace treaty following defeat in World War I. The definitive turning point occurred in 1926, the year in which the Treaty of Versailles expired and a complete revival in commercial aviation began. Paradoxically, the symbol of Germany's new aeronautical strength became that of Deutsche Lufthansa, the new official airline, formally established on January 6, 1926, with the merger of Junkers Luftverkehr and Deutscher Aero Lloyd. Backed by massive government support, DHL proved to be the most active and enterprising of the European airlines. Its success was not only commercial, however. In practice, the expansion of civilian aviation had a direct effect on the aeronautical industry which, by now free from restrictions, launched the production of relatively advanced aircraft and found itself provided with an opportunity to reconstruct a complete technical, organizational, and operative structure that would soon take on a military guise.

This deceptive process had unexpectedly gathered speed after Adolf Hitler came to power in 1933, and even after its official foundation, the new air force continued to use civilian aviation as a screen for its own activities. Many of the aircraft that were to constitute the backbone of the Luftwaffe in the following years first appeared bearing the insignia of commercial airlines: from the Junkers Ju.52 to the Ju.86, from the Heinkel He.111 to the Dornier Do.17. If the origin of these bombers was deceptive, there was much less reticence as far as the fighters were concerned: the Messerschmitt Bf.109 even took part in important sporting events, thus publicizing its remarkable performance.

During the Spanish Civil War, the opportunity of trying out this war machine's potential in action was not lacking. An air force, the Condor Legion, was formed specifically for this purpose and was sent to support the Nationalists. In the course of more than two years fighting, it served to test the entire arsenal of the Luftwaffe. This experience stimulated preparation for World War II, and when the attack on Poland took place, in September 1939, Hitler could count on the world's most powerful air force (its frontline consisted of 4,840 of the most advanced and competitive aircraft, including 1,750 bombers and 1,200 fighters), fed by an industrial network that was already producing 1,000 aircraft a month and that would produce 8,300 of all kinds in 1939 alone.

Chronology

1938

February 25. The prototype of the Blohm und Voss Bv.141 takes to the air. This original reconnaissance aircraft was rejected by the Luftwaffe.

March. A Dornier Do.18 seaplane bearing the insignia of Deutsche Lufthansa breaks the straight distance flying record for its category, covering 5,211 miles (8,392 km) in 43 hours. The military version of this aircraft went into service in the Luftwaffe in September.

August. Maiden flight of the Dornier Do.217 V1 prototype, derived from the Do.17, which was to go into service toward the end of 1940. Up to June 1944, 1,541 bomber and 364 night-fighter versions of this two-engine aircraft were built.

1939

May. The first two-engine Heinkel He.111 Hs go into service. This was the bomber's major production variant and approximately 5,000 were built. By September, more than 800 were operative.

February. Maiden flight of the Blohm und Voss Bv.138 prototype, one of Germany's most effective naval reconnaissance planes. The aircraft went into service toward the end of 1940.

March 30. A Heinkel He.100 V8 monoplane, a modified variant of the fighter built to compete with the Messerschmitt Bf.109, breaks the world speed record piloted by Ernst Udet, reaching 463.642 mph (746.606 km/h). Despite this remarkable performance, the aircraft was not adopted by the Luftwaffe.

April 26. Another German aircraft breaks a speed record: the Messerschmitt Me.209 V1, an experimental aircraft built specially for this purpose and piloted by Fritz Wendel, reaches 468.940 mph (755.138 km/h). This category record was to remain unbroken until August 1969.

June 1. The prototype of the Focke Wulf Fw.190 V1, the Luftwaffe's second most important fighter, takes to the air. It went into service in July 1941, 13,367 of the interceptor and 6,634 of the fighter-bomber versions being built in all.

August 27. The first aircraft in the world to be powered by a turbojet, the Heinkel He.178, fitted with an 838 lb (380 kg) thrust HeS 3b engine designed and tuned by Pabst von Ohain, takes to the air. The aircraft did not go into service, but it lay the foundations for the experiences that were to lead to the creation of future German jet combat planes.

September 26. The Junkers Ju.88 A-1, one of the most versatile and widely used German bombers of the entire war, commences its operative career. From 1939 to 1945, more than 16,000 were built in dozens of versions. Serving in many roles, they constituted the backbone of the Luftwaffe.

November 19. The prototype of the Heinkel He.177, the first and only heavy bomber to be built in Germany, makes its maiden flight. Its preparation was to be long and laborious, due mainly to the unusual arrangement of its four engines (placed in pairs and driving a single propeller). Of the approximately 1,000 that were built, only a couple of hundred were used in combat, with little success.

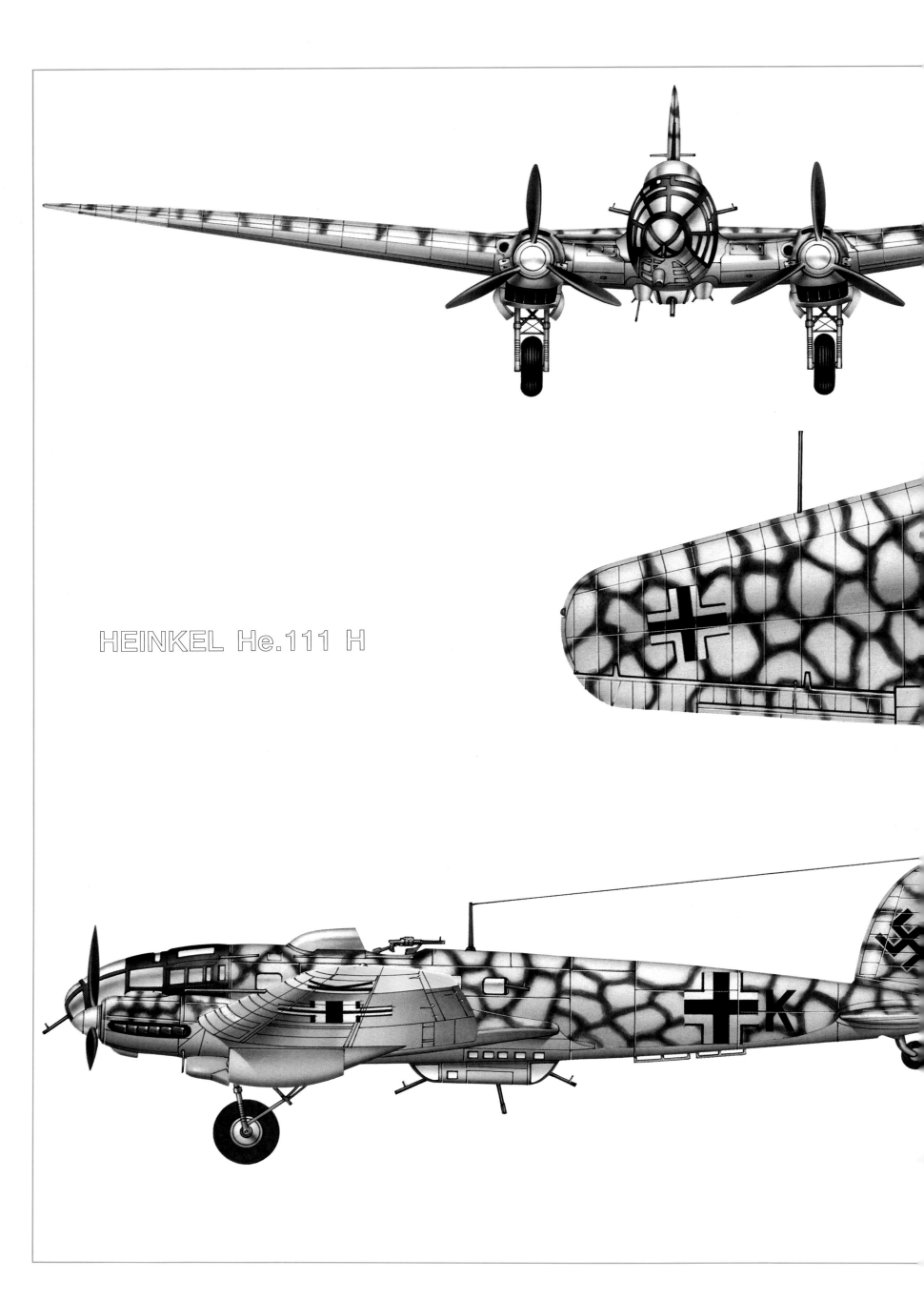

HEINKEL He.111 H

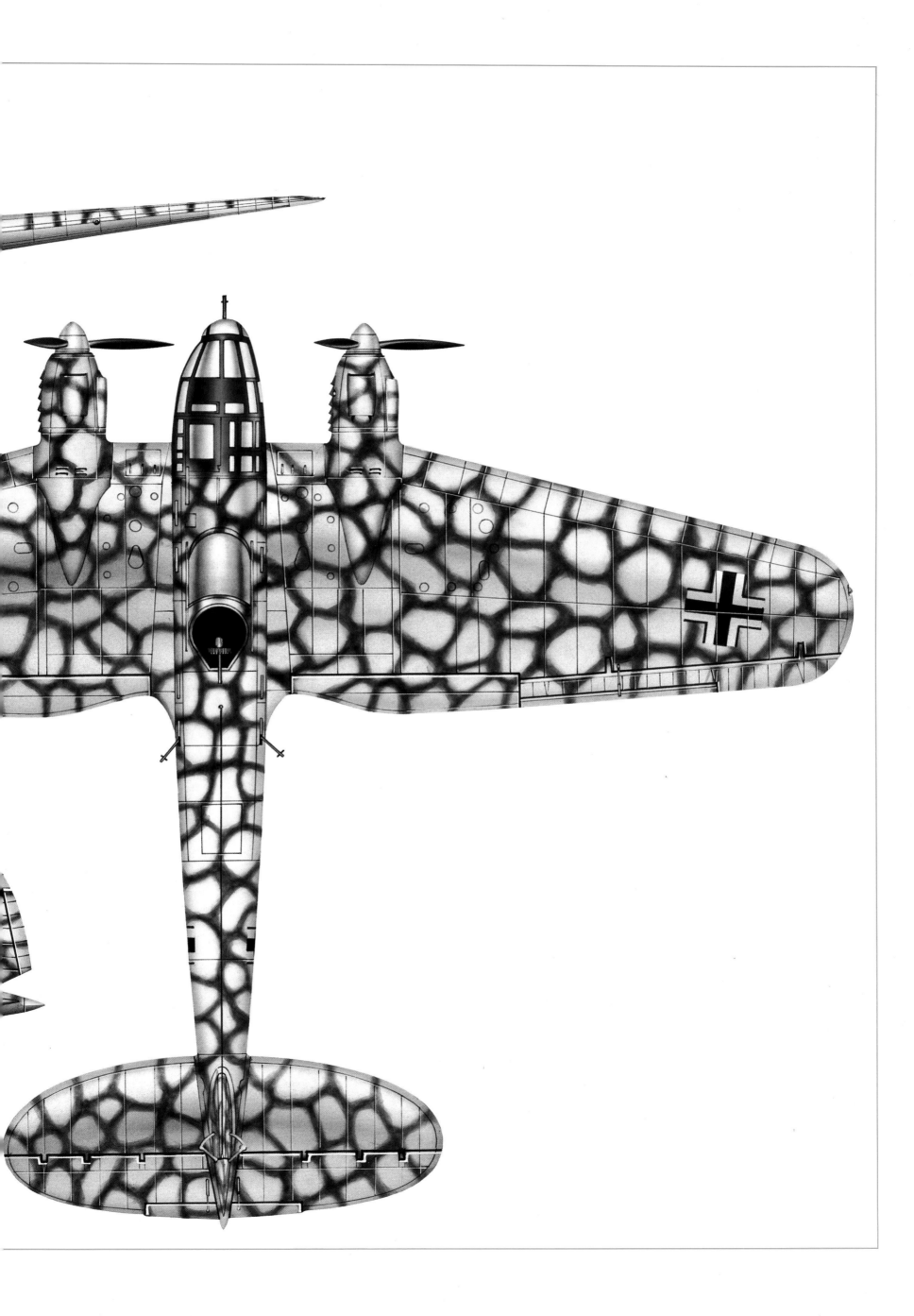

HEINKEL He.111

Officially designed as a civilian aircraft (in the same way as its contemporaries, the Junkers Ju.86 and the Dornier Do.17), the Heinkel He.111 was perhaps the best representative of the deceptive rearmament policy carried out by Germany in the early 1930s. Like the other two aircraft, it was created to fulfill the double role of fast commercial transport plane and bomber, but it was eventually to stand out for its true qualities as a combat plane more than the other two. This occurred especially at a quantitative level, considering that production of this elegant two-engine aircraft continued from 1936 virtually up to the end of the war, totaling more than 7,300 in numerous variants. These were operational on all fronts in a variety of roles, proving the initial project's great qualities even in the presence of more modern and battle-hardened models.

The first prototype of the He.111 took to the air on February 24, 1935. The aircraft was clearly inspired by the single-engine He.70, although it was notably larger. It was followed by another two prototypes, with a shorter wingspan, and the fourth prototype became the progenitor of the civilian version, capable of carrying 10 passengers and a postal load. The aircraft was presented on January 10, 1936, and 10 planes were built, designated He.111 C. These went into regular service with Lufthansa by the end of the year.

Following the disappointing performance of the third prototype (designed for military use), at the beginning of 1936, a fifth experimental aircraft appeared and led to the creation of the first bomber variant, the He.111 B. Characterized by the use of two Daimler Benz DB 600 engines, these aircraft went into service at the end of the year, and, in February 1937, 30 or so were assigned to the Condor Legion in Spain, where they formed the nucleus of what was to become a large force. On the assembly lines, the military versions soon followed one after another. After only a few D series aircraft had been completed, a shortage of Daimler Benz engines led to the development of the successive He.111 E variant of 1938, in which Junkers Jumo 211 engines were used. The He.111 G was characterized by substantial modifications to the wing structure, but it was in 1938, with the appearance of the prototypes of the P and H series, that the bomber assumed its definitive configuration. In these aircraft, the front part of the fuselage was redesigned. It was completely glazed and blended into the rest of the structure, assuming the characteristic asymmetrical form in order to allow the pilot maximum visibility.

The He.111 Hs (in which the Jumo engine was used definitively, in increasingly powerful versions) became the major production variant: these aircraft went into service in May 1939, and more than 800 were operational by September; approximately 5,000 were to come off the production lines, in many versions. After the H-2 and the H-3, one of the most widely used was the He.111 H-6, which appeared in 1941, specially designed for naval warfare and used with great success in the role of torpedo launcher. The 1943 H-10 and H-12 variants were characterized by the increase in their bomb loads (the Heinkel He.111 H-12 could launch two radio-controlled Henschel Hs.293 missiles), while the bomb load in the H-16 series reached 7,174 lb (3,250 kg). The final H-23 version appeared in 1944 and was destined for the launching of parachutists. Lastly, mention of 10 He.111 Zs should be made. In reality, these consisted of two H-6 airframes joined by means of a new central wing trunk in which a fifth engine was installed. These aircraft were designed to tow the massive Messerschmitt Me.321 transport glider.

The Heinkel's career lasted well beyond World War II. In Spain, 263 of the H-16 variant were built on license by CASA, and they remained in service throughout the 1960s.

---

color plate
Heinkel He.111 H II/KG 53 Condor Legion - USSR 1941

Aircraft:	Heinkel He.111 H-2
Nation:	Germany
Manufacturer:	Ernst Heinkel AG
Type:	Bomber
Year:	1939
Engine:	2 Junkers Jumo 211A-3, 12-cylinder V, liquid-cooled, 1,100 hp each
Wingspan:	74 ft 1 in (22.60 m)
Length:	53 ft 9 in (16.39 m)
Height:	13 ft 1 in (4.00 m)
Weight:	30,865 lb (14,000 kg) loaded
Maximum speed:	252 mph (405 km/h)
Ceiling:	27,900 ft (8,500 m)
Range:	1,280 miles (2,060 km)
Armament:	6 machine guns; 5,501 lb (2,495 kg) of bombs
Crew:	5

Heinkel He.111 in service on the Russian front with additional external bomb load.

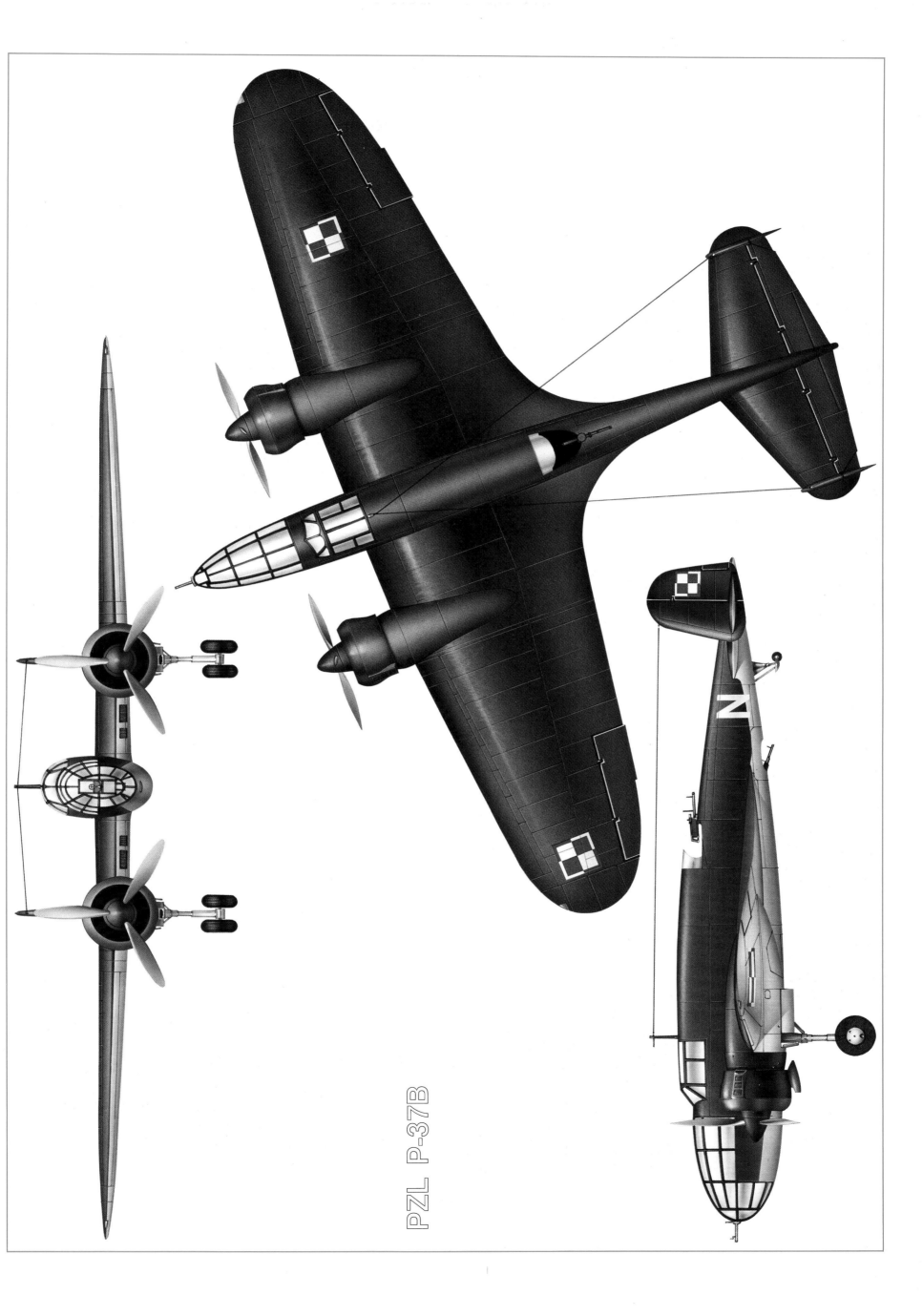

PZL P-37B

PZL P-37

Paradoxically, the PZL P-37, the most modern aircraft in service in the Polish air force when the war broke out, was never produced in any great quantity. The fate of this elegant, two-engine bomber was decided by the members of the General Staff who, after heated argument, gave priority to the construction of other types of aircraft. As a result, only a few months before the outbreak of the war, production programs were reduced by a third, and only 36 of the final P-37B version were operational at the time of the German invasion.

In the period between the two wars, the development of a home-produced multiengine bomber had been slowed down in Poland, due mainly to high production costs. At the beginning of the 1930s, the Aeronautical Department had once again rejected a sound proposal presented by PZL (regarding the PZL-3 model) and had preferred to order 20 or so three-engine Fokker F.VIIb/3ms transformed into bombers. It was the need to replace these obsolete aircraft, clearly unsuitable for military duties, that caused PZL to proceed with new studies to be submitted for examination by the Aeronautical Department.

The first proposal was for a bomber version of the PZL 30 civilian transport plane, which had not found any buyers; the second and rather more valid proposal was presented in July 1934 and aroused considerable interest. It was a project for a modern, low-wing monoplane, quite advanced from an aerodynamic and structural point of view and powered by a pair of Bristol Pegasus radial engines. In April 1935, the military authorities gave permission for the construction of three prototypes, the first of which took to the air at the end of June 1936, with the designation P-37/1. The series of flight tests revealed the excellent performance of the aircraft and, after a number of structural modifications, the bomber went into production on the basis of an initial order for 30 aircraft, designated P-37A. The first 10 had a single tail fin empennage, while the remaining 20 were characterized by double tail planes, a configuration similar to that tested on the second prototype (P-37/II), in which a more powerful version of the Pegasus engine had been used (925 hp as compared to 873 hp in the previous series).

The P-37A was presented at the Belgrade Air Show and at the Paris Aeronautical Salon in 1938, and it aroused great interest, orders being obtained from Bulgaria, Yugoslavia, Rumania, and Turkey for a total of 75 aircraft. However, these orders were never fulfilled, due to the outbreak of the war. The P-37As were delivered to the units of the Polish air force from the spring of 1938. In the meantime, from the second prototype a second production variant had been developed (P-37B), characterized by modifications to the canopy and to the landing gear, in addition to the use of more powerful engines. Deliveries of these aircraft (on the basis of an initial order for 150) commenced toward the end of the year, and on consignment the P-37As were relegated to training.

At this point, the contrast of opinions within the General Staff led to the orders being cut drastically and to a consequent slowing down of production. The 150 P-37Bs were reduced to 100, and barely 70 of these had been delivered by the time the war broke out.

The war also halted the development of a more powerful version of the bomber, the P-49, characterized by the use of 1,600 hp engines. A prototype was at an advanced stage of completion, but its construction was suspended because of the advance of the German troops. The aircraft was destroyed.

color plate
PZL P-37B Polish Air Force - Poland 1939

Aircraft:	P-37B
Nation:	Poland
Manufacturer:	Parstwowe Zaklady Lotnicze
Type:	Attack
Year:	1938
Engine:	2 PZL-Bristol Pegasus XX, 9-cylinder radial, air-cooled, 918 hp each
Wingspan:	58 ft 10 in (17.93 m)
Length:	42 ft 5 in (12.92 m)
Height:	16 ft 8 in (5.08 m)
Weight:	18,872 lb (8,560 kg) loaded
Maximum speed:	276 mph (445 km/h) at 11,154 ft (3,400 m)
Ceiling:	19,680 ft (6,000 m)
Range:	932 miles (1,500 km)
Armament:	3 machine guns; 5,688 lb (2,580 kg) of bombs
Crew:	4

The prototype of the PZL P-37.

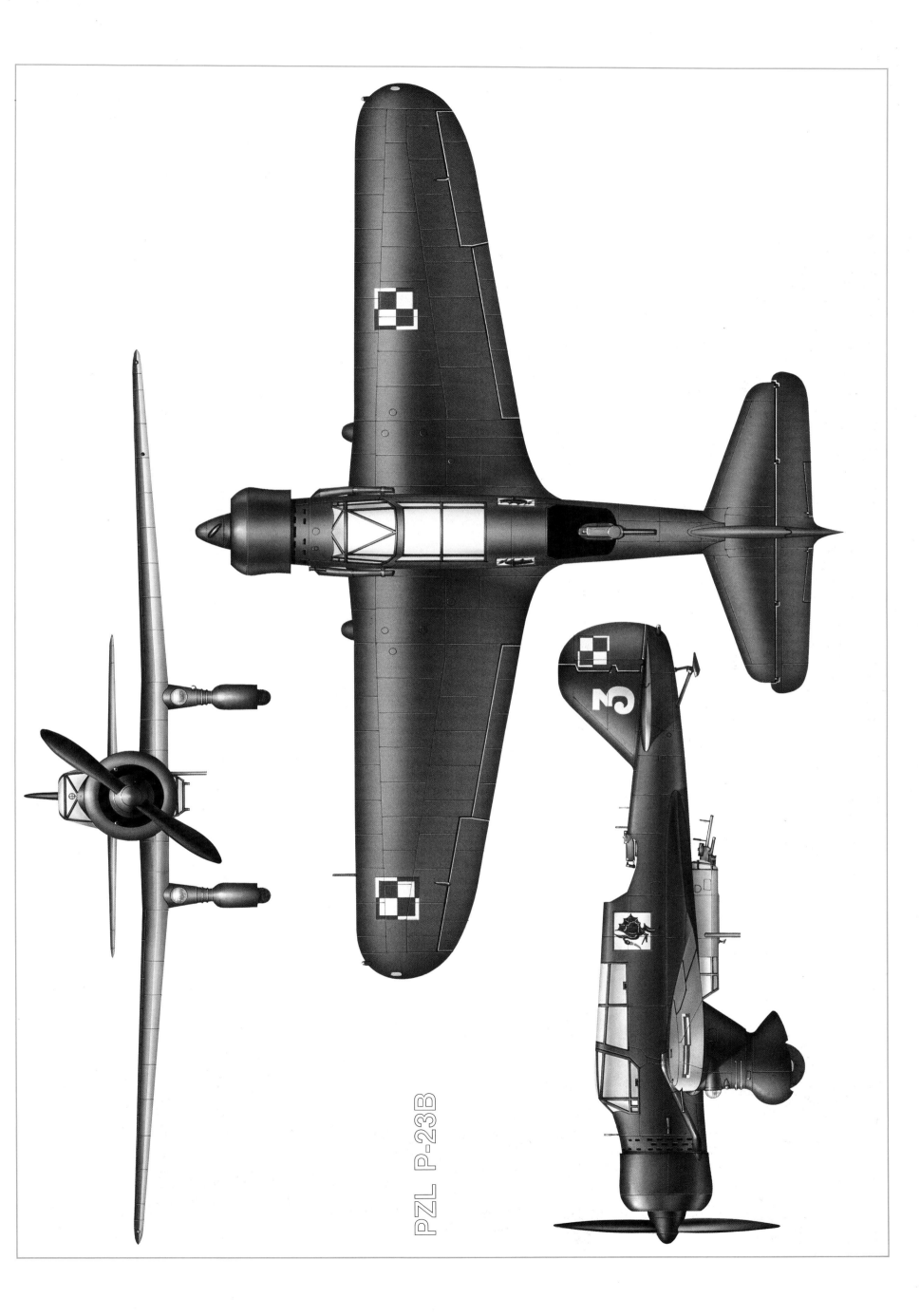

PZL P-23B

In the period between the two wars, the Polish air force attributed as much importance to the tactical support units designed to operate in close cooperation with ground forces, as it did to the fighter units. This practice, which dated back to the experiences of the conflict fought in 1919/20 against the Soviet Union, was maintained throughout the 1930s. The PZL P-23 *Karas* was a typical example of this philosophy: designed in 1932, it entered service toward the middle of 1937, and 250 aircraft were built in two main versions. When World War II broke out, this robust monoplane attack aircraft equipped 12 front-line units and, in the brief period of combat against the Germans, it proved to be an effective weapon.

The specifications that led to the creation of the PZL P-23 were issued by the Polish military authorities in 1931, with the aim of developing a home-produced aircraft to replace those of French origin (especially the Potez and Breguet XIX biplanes) in service in the tactical support units. At that time, PZL designed a single-engine commercial transport plane (designated P-13) that it intended to offer to LOT, the state airline. It was an all-metal low-wing monoplane, capable of carrying six passengers, and its designer (Stanislaw Prauss) intended that it should replace the Junkers F-13 then in service. However, despite the project's promising characteristics, LOT did not show excessive interest, and work on it was abandoned toward the end of 1931.

At this point, Prauss decided to propose his P-13 to the military authorities, offering it as a basis for the development of a new three-seater tactical support plane, and a series of consultations went ahead, culminating in the general approval of the project in the spring of 1932. A Bristol Pegasus radial engine, built on license by Skoda, was chosen, and, in the fall, an order was made for the construction of four prototypes, one of which was to be used for static tests. However, the development phase proved to be rather long, and it was not until August 1934 that the first P-23, powered by a 590 hp engine that drove a two-bladed wooden propeller, was able to make its maiden flight. During a series of tests, it became necessary to carry out a number of modifications (especially of a structural nature) and these were incorporated into the two successive flying prototypes. The definitive configuration was not reached until 1935, when the aircraft went into production on the basis of an order for 40 planes of the initial P-25A version and 210 of the second variant (P-23B). The latter was characterized by the use of a 680 hp Pegasus VIII engine.

The first *Karas* A took to the air in June 1936, but production was slowed down by engine problems, and in the end the aircraft that were completed were destined for use as trainers. In the fall of the same year, deliveries of the more efficient P-23B model began, and it became operative from the middle of the following year. By the end of 1937, 200 of these aircraft had been built, and to these were added another 10 ordered later.

During production of the *Karas*, studies for developing the basic model began. A P-23B was modified structurally (the most obvious variation was the use of a two tail plane empennage) and, redesignated the P-42, it was used for the creation of an even further improved version, the P-46. However, both these aircraft remained at an experimental stage. The same did not occur to a subsequent version (similar to the *Karas* B, but with a more powerful engine and armament) that went into production as the P-43A, on the basis of an order from Bulgaria for 12 aircraft. Another variant was derived from this aircraft (the P-43B, powered by a 980 hp Gnome-Rhône engine), 42 of which were ordered, again by Bulgaria. However, only 33 aircraft had been delivered by August 1939. The rest were requisitioned by the Polish air force when the war broke out.

color plate
PZL P-23B 22nd Bomber Squadron Polish Air Force - Poland 1939

Aircraft:	PZL P-23B
Nation:	Poland
Manufacturer:	Panstwowe Zaklady Lotnicze
Type:	Attack
Year:	1937
Engine:	PZL-Bristol Pegasus VIII, 9-cylinder radial, air-cooled, 680 hp
Wingspan:	45 ft 9 $^1/_2$ in (13.95 m)
Length:	31 ft 9 $^1/_2$ in (9.68 m)
Height:	10 ft 10 in (3.30 m)
Weight:	7,773 lb (3,526 kg) loaded
Maximum speed:	198 mph (319 km/h) at 11,975 ft (3,650 m)
Ceiling:	23,950 ft (7,300 m)
Range:	782 miles (1,260 km)
Armament:	2 machine guns; 1,543 lb (700 kg) of bombs
Crew:	3

Rumanian air force PZL P-23 during a combat mission on the Russian front.

THE NETHERLANDS
POLAND
YUGOSLAVIA

On September 1, 1939, Poland was the first country to suffer attack by the Germans, and the outbreak of hostilities struck its military aviation at the time in which it was beginning to reap the benefits of a vast strengthening program. This provided for the creation of 102 combat units, with a force of 960 aircraft, by April 1942. These were to include 22 ground cooperation units (with 220 aircraft), 30 fighter units (330 aircraft), 15 attack units (165 twin-engine aircraft), and 15 bomber units (105 aircraft). However, this program had gone ahead very slowly, so much so that in 1939 production reached its lowest level ever, with only 215 aircraft of all types (including civilian models) being delivered by September. Despite all this, at the time the invasion occurred, most of the approximately 900 front-line aircraft were still clearly inferior to those of the Germans, and the valiant struggle put up by the PZL fighters to halt the onslaught of the Luftwaffe and the Wehrmacht was in vain. The approximately 430 operative aircraft were subdivided into 15 fighter units (114 aircraft), four bomber units (36 aircraft), and 12 observation units (84 aircraft); in all, 43 units with 392 combat planes, plus 36 unarmed reconnaissance aircraft and 9 transport planes. This force was virtually destroyed during operations: a total of almost 330 aircraft were destroyed, while the Luftwaffe lost 258, with another 263 seriously damaged. Following the invasion, many Polish pilots sought refuge in France and Great Britain, where they played a distinguished role, above all in the Battle of Britain.

Nine months later, the situation in the Netherlands was very similar. In this small nation with a great aeronautical tradition, military aviation had become an autonomous armed force on November 1, 1938. Production was at a very high level, thanks to the intense activity of Fokker, and the D.XXI and G.1 could be considered the equals of any adversary. However, these aircraft went into service too late in the units of an air force that appeared extremely unsuited to face the strength of its adversary. On May 10, 1940, barely 126 aircraft were operational in the Dutch military aviation. During the few days of combat, they were practically all destroyed, although not before having shot down 50 German planes.

As for Yugoslavia, its air force was still clearly out of date at the time of the invasion, despite the appearance of some excellent projects (such as the Rogorzarsty IK-3 fighter) for these aircraft were, still in an operative evaluation phase, in a dozen or so examples in the summer of 1940. At the time of the German attack on April 6, 1941, the Yugoslavian military aviation consisted of approximately 600 aircraft, almost all of which were out of date.

Their brave resistance served only to postpone the moment of surrender, twelve days later (April 17). Many Yugoslavian pilots continued the struggle in the ranks of the Royal Air Force, although others chose to fight for the Axis forces and joined the Croatian air force.

Chronology

1938

Autumn. Deliveries of the PZL P-37B, the most modern bomber produced by the Polish aeronautical industry, commence. However, this valid twin-engine aircraft was to be built in totally insufficient numbers: only 36 were in service at the time of the German invasion.

November. In Yugoslavia an order is issued for 12 production series Rogozarski IK-3 fighters. The prototype had taken to the air in the spring, revealing the excellent qualities of its performance, so much so as to be considered competitive with the German Messerschmitt Bf.109E and the British Hurricane Mk.I. At the time of the German attack, only six IK-3s were operational.

1939

April 11. The first production series Fokker G.1A comes off the assembly lines and is tested in flight. The units of the Dutch air force received the aircraft from July: 36 in all. Only 23 planes could be considered operative on May 10, 1940.

June. The prototype of the Fokker D.XXIII, one of the most interesting fighter projects created in the years immediately prior to the war, takes to the air. Characterized by the use of two engines (one tractor and one thrust) and by double tail beams, this aircraft was plagued by tuning problems. The war put an end to its development.

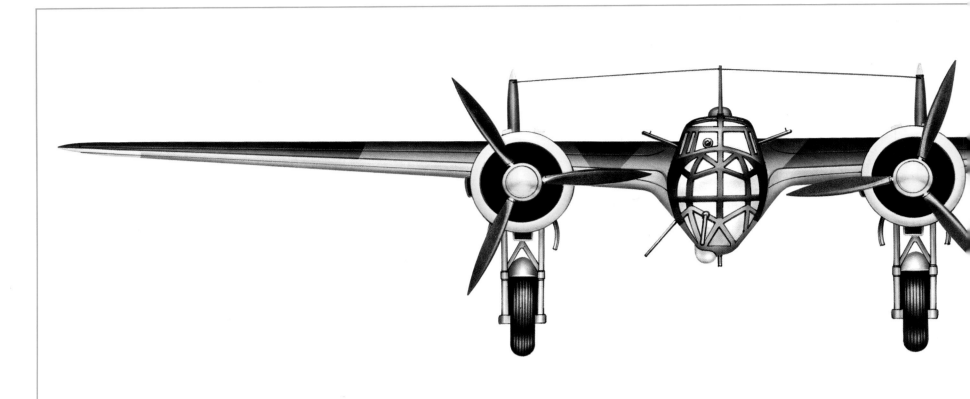

DORNIER Do.17 Z-2

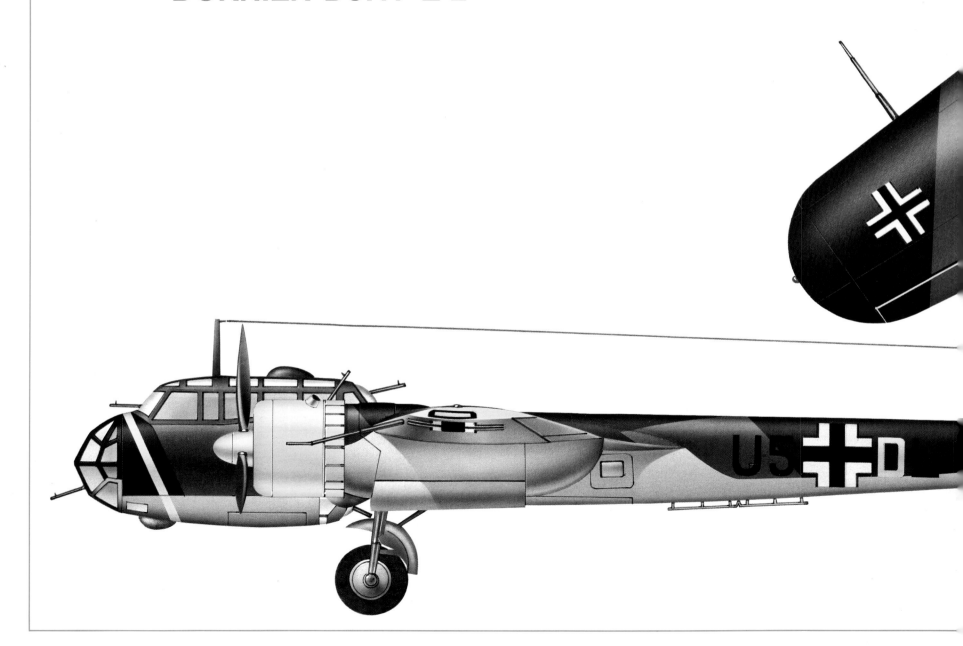

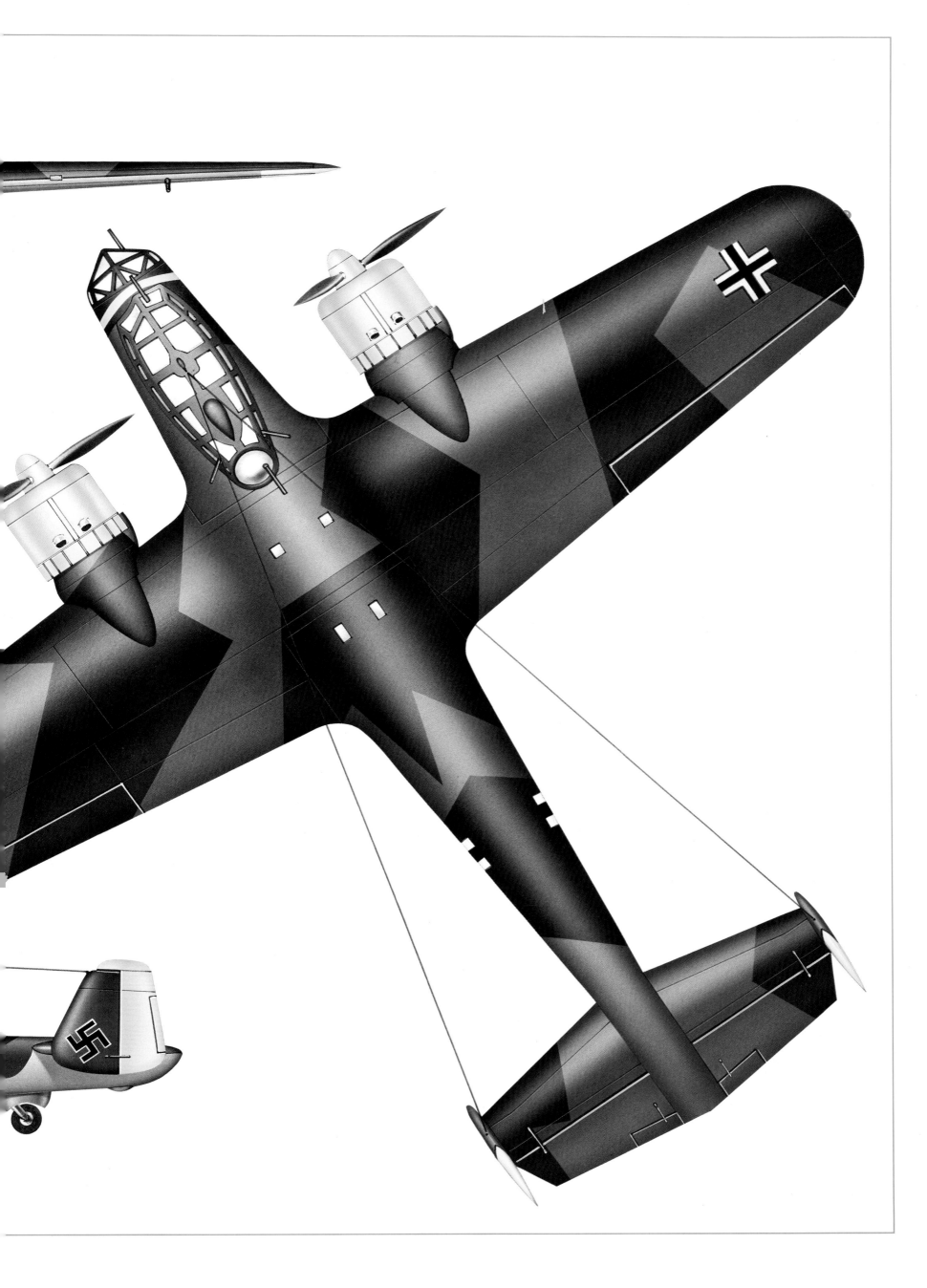

Together with the Junkers Ju.86 and the Heinkel He.111, the Dornier Do.17 was one of the products of the deceptive policy of rearmament carried out by Germany. This fast and elegant two-engine aircraft originated in the first half of the 1930s, in response to a request by Deutsche Lufthansa for the construction of a fast postal plane capable of carrying six passengers, but it found its true dimension in the role of bomber. It was, in fact, as a combat plane that the Do.17 went down in aviation history, one of the Luftwaffe's best known and most widely used in battle. It was an aircraft that, in a continuous evolution composed of numerous series, versions, and derivatives, remained in production for the entire duration of the war and operated on practically all fronts.

The project was begun in 1933, and three prototypes were completed in the course of the following year. However, after evaluations, these aircraft were not considered suitable for commercial use (one of the reasons being that the fuselage was too narrow, preventing the passengers from being housed comfortably), and they were sent back to the manufacturer. Nevertheless, the potential of the aircraft remained great, and it was immediately transformed for military use. The fourth prototype, which appeared in the summer of 1935, became the founder of a long series of bombers, whose initial production series (the E-1 and the F-1, the latter being for reconnaissance) received their baptism of fire in Spain, as part of the Condor Legion, in 1937.

Apart from the advanced nature of its layout (all-metal, mid-wing monoplane with retractable landing gear and carefully designed from the point of view of aerodynamics), the most modern feature of the Dornier Do.17 lay in its performance, and more especially in its speed. A sensational demonstration of this was provided by the victory gained by one of the prototypes in the 1937 Alps Circuit, a race held in Zurich for military aircraft, during which it proved to be the fastest of all the fighters then in production.

After a series of minor variations in which attempts were made to improve and to optimize the features on the project, the most widely produced variant was the Z, which went into service in 1939 and of which just over 500 were built up to the summer of 1940. This series, as well as being the last model before the switch to the 217 type (larger and more powerful), incorporated substantial modifications as compared to the previous ones, particularly in the structure and in the configuration of the front part of the fuselage. This was deepened (in order to increase the efficiency of the rear ventral defensive position) and was almost completely glazed, with the aim of improving the bombardier's position. In particular, in the Do.17 Z-2 series, the use of more powerful power plants (two 1,000 hp BMW Bramo radial engines) made it possible to increase the defensive armament to eight machine guns and the offensive armament to a ton of bombs.

Other variants of particular interest were the Z-6 and Z-10, conceived as night bombers and fitted with heavy armament concentrated entirely in the nose (three machine guns and a 20 mm cannon in the Do.17 Z-6 and four machine guns and two cannons in the Do.17 Z-10). Although the few aircraft built did not have an extensive operational career, they made a valuable contribution to the development of techniques for this particular type of combat.

At the outbreak of the conflict, 370 Do.17s were in service in the Luftwaffe, of which two-thirds belonged to the Z series, and these aircraft took part in all operations during the first two years of the war. Although they were good aircraft overall, they were not particularly outstanding, lacking the bomb-load capacity of the Heinkel He.111 and the speed of the Junkers Ju.88. The Do.17s were withdrawn from front-line service toward the end of 1942, replaced by the more powerful and efficient Do.217s, and were gradually relegated to secondary roles.

color plate
Dornier Do.17 Z-2 3/KG 2 Holzhammer - Balkans 1941

A Dornier Do.17 with blacked-out insignia during the Battle of Britain.

Do.17s of the 3rd Kampf Geschwader flying toward targets in French territory in 1940.

Aircraft:	Dornier Do.17 Z-2
Nation:	Germany
Manufacturer:	Dornier-Werke GmbH
Type:	Bomber
Year:	1939
Engine:	2 BMW Bramo 323P, 9-cylinder radial, air-cooled, 1,000 hp each
Wingspan:	59 ft (18.00 m)
Length:	51 ft 10 in (15.79 m)
Height:	14 ft 11 $\frac{1}{2}$ in (4.55 m)
Weight:	18,930 lb (8,590 kg) loaded
Maximum speed:	255 mph (410 km/h) at 13,120 ft (4,000 m)
Ceiling:	26,900 ft (8,200 m)
Range:	721 miles (1,160 km)
Armament:	6/8 machine guns; 2,200 lb (1,000 kg) of bombs
Crew:	4

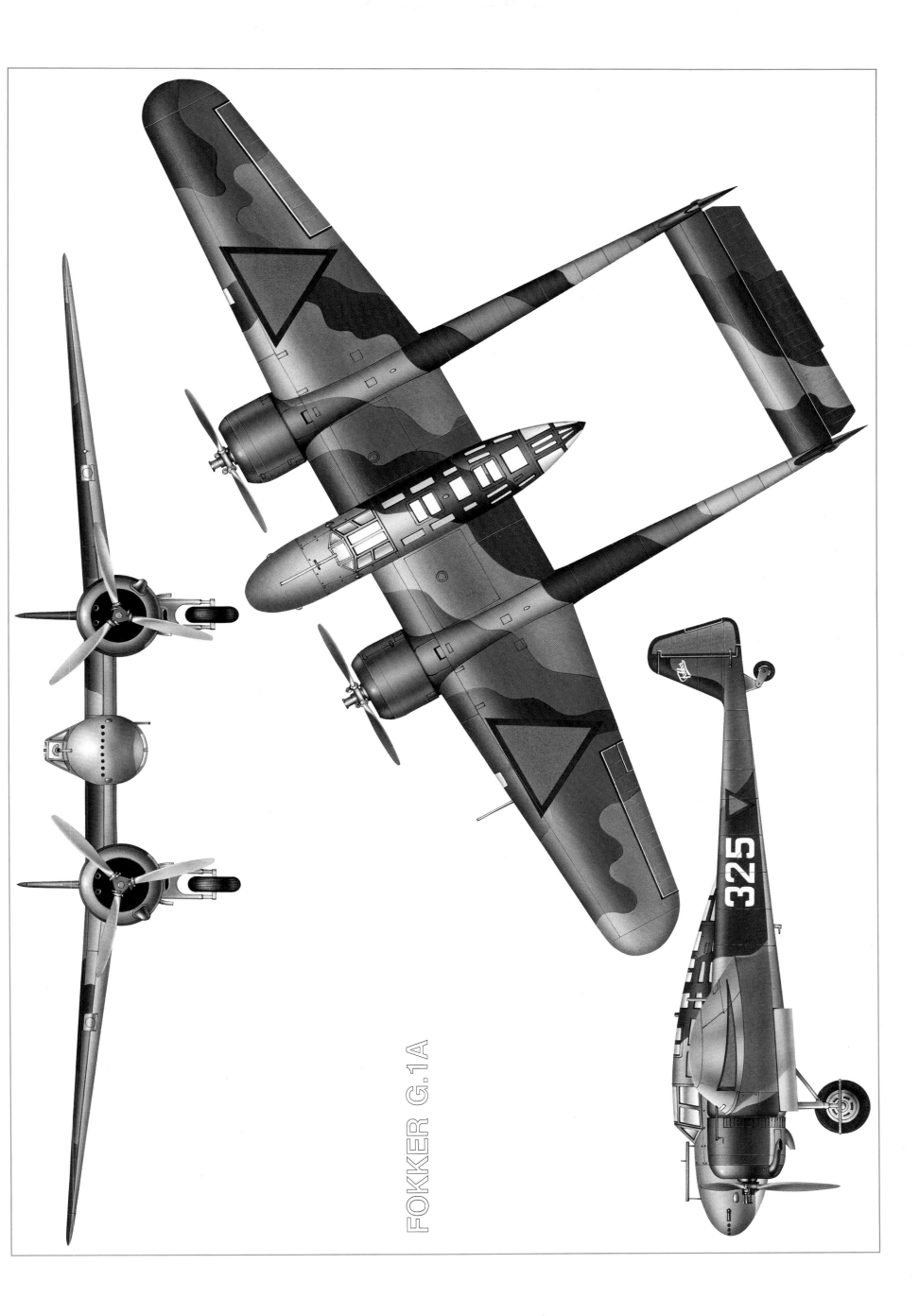

FOKKER G.1A

Two cannons and two fixed machine guns in the nose, plus another flexible one installed in the rear, as well as performance that included a maximum speed of over 280 mph (450 km/h). Aside from the advanced concept of its general layout, it was these characteristics that most impressed observers when the prototype of the Fokker G.1 appeared at the Paris Aeronautical Salon in 1936.

This was a two-engine middle-wing aircraft with retractable landing gear and an original configuration in the double tail beams and the central fuselage. It was used to best advantage as a fighter, but was created to carry out other roles, such as that of fighter-bomber or reconnaissance plane, with equal efficiency. The Dutch air force received 36 of the G.1A version in 1939, of which 23 were operational on May 10, 1940, when the German invasion began. In the course of five days of combat, these aircraft were destroyed, either in the air or on the ground. However, production of the G.1A also included a variant destined for export (designated the G.1B) and totaled 62 aircraft in all. Twenty or so G.1Bs, which formed part of a lot originally destined for Finland, were requisitioned by the Germans and used for training. In May 1941, one of these allowed two Fokker test pilots to make an adventurous escape from Schipol and to reach the English coast.

With the G.1 project, Fokker had intended to launch an entirely new generation of combat aircraft. Work on the prototype commenced in great secrecy in 1934, and tests began after the Paris show. The prototype took to the air for the first time on March 16, 1937.

The aircraft was of mixed construction: the airframe of the front part of the fuselage consisted of steel tubes with aluminum covering, whereas the central part was built of wood and the rear section (which was widely glazed) of light alloy. The wing was entirely of wood, while the two tail beams were all-metal, except for the vertical rudders, which had a canvas covering. The landing gear retracted into the engine nacelles. The prototype was powered by two Hispano-Suiza 80-02 radial engines capable of generating 750 hp at altitude.

During tests some changes were introduced, and when an order was placed for 36 aircraft in November 1937, the military authorities requested that the engine be replaced by two 830 hp Bristol Mercury VIII engines, which were to drive the three-bladed variable pitch metal propellers, and that the fixed armament be changed to eight 7.9 mm machine guns. In addition, the installation of a bomb load of 660 lb (300 kg) was planned. The standard crew consisted of two men, although the first four aircraft had been built to carry a third crew member.

These aircraft were designated G.1A, and production went ahead at a slow rate, due to delays in engine deliveries. The first of the series was not flight tested until April 11, 1939, and units began to receive the planes in July.

In the meantime, Fokker had developed a second version of the G.1, destined for export. This differed from the first in its slightly reduced dimensions, its armament, and in the adoption of two 750 hp Pratt & Whitney Twin Wasp jr. SB4-G engines. In 1939, Fokker G.1Bs were ordered by Finland (26 aircraft), by Sweden (18), by Denmark (which planned to produce them on license), by Spain, and by Estonia (9). The outbreak of the war halted production: only 12 G.1Bs, part of the Finnish order, had been completed. Three of these were provided with armament and fought against the Luftwaffe. The rest were requisitioned by the Germans.

---

color plate

Fokker G.1A 4th Fighter Group Dutch Army Air Corps - The Netherlands 1940.

A Fokker G.1 adapted for reconnaissance with the addition of a glazed ventral pod.

A Dutch air force Fokker G.1A in prewar camouflage and markings.

Aircraft:	Fokker G.1A
Nation:	The Netherlands
Manufacturer:	Fokker
Type:	Fighter
Year:	1939
Engine:	2 Bristol Mercury VIII, 9-cylinder radial, air-cooled, 830 hp
Wingspan:	56 ft 3 in (17.15 m)
Length:	37 ft 9 in (11.50 m)
Height:	11 ft 2 in (3.40 m)
Weight:	10,582 lb (4,970 kg) loaded
Maximum speed:	295 mph (475 km/h)
Ceiling:	30,500 ft (9,300 m)
Range:	876 miles (1,409 km)
Armament:	8/9 machine guns; 660 lb (300 kg) of bombs
Crew:	2/3

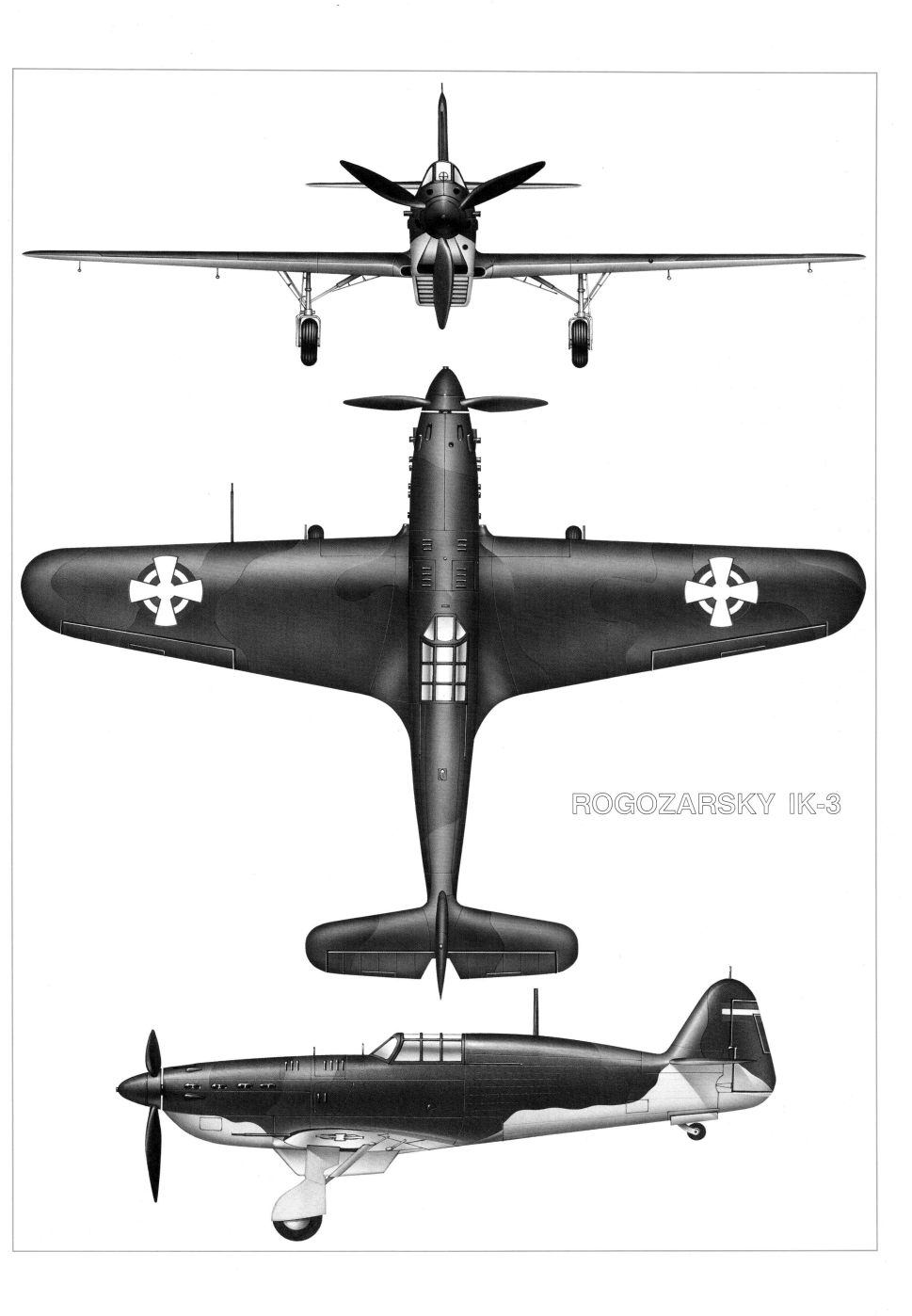

ROGOZARSKY IK-3

ROGOZARSKI IK-3

The innovative processes that were linked to the change from biplane to monoplane reached the Yugoslavian aeronautical industry, traditionally considered second-rate compared to those of the major European powers, in the first half of the 1930s. The result of this was the Rogozarski IK-3, a small, agile fighter with enclosed cockpit and all retractable landing gear, which proved to be just as reliable and rather more easy to handle than its two more illustrious contemporaries, the British Hawker Hurricane and the German Messerschmitt Bf.109. However, the IK-3 had a relatively short life span, dictated by the events of the war itself: the production program came to a halt when the Germans invaded, by which time only 12 aircraft had been delivered to the units.

In 1933, the idea of developing a modern combat plane came to Ljubomir Ilic and Kosta Sivcev, the two technicians who had produced the first entirely Yugoslavian fighter, the IK-1, a couple of years earlier. Encouraged by this experience, the two designers were convinced that the era of the biplane and the high-wing monoplane was over and that, considering the high-quality performance of the new bombers being developed at the time, only a low-wing monoplane with retractable landing gear possessed the characteristics necessary to guarantee supremacy in the air. The project got under way in great secrecy, and toward mid 1936 all drawings and documentation were handed over to the military authorities for examination.

However, the initial evaluation phase proved to be long, the delay caused to a great extent by official skepticism concerning the new formula. Not until March of the following year was a contract signed for the production of a prototype. The factory that was to supervise its construction was Rogozarski, based in Belgrade. The first aircraft was completed a year later, and the IK-3 made its maiden flight near the end of May 1938. The fuselage had a steel tube airframe with a mixed canvas and metal covering, and the wing was built almost entirely of wood, with only a few steel tube reinforcements. The prototype was powered by a 910 hp "V-12" Hispano-Suiza 12 Y29 engine with supercharger (although in the production series this was replaced by the equally powerful 12 Ycrs model built by Avia on license), which drove a three-bladed variable pitch metal propeller. The armament consisted of a 20 mm cannon installed on the propeller shaft and two fixed machine guns in the fuselage.

During evaluation tests, the concentration of the armament in the nose was one of the most appreciated features, although the aircraft's maneuverability and excellent overall performance also made a good impression. However, flight tests were interrupted suddenly on January 19, 1939, when the prototype crashed to the ground following a deep dive, causing the death of the test pilot, Milan Pokorni. Even though the causes of the accident were not attributed to serious structural problems, this event delayed still further the start of production, which had been planned on the basis of an order for 12 aircraft barely three months earlier.

The first six aircraft were delivered in March 1940, and the others by July. Beginning on April 6, 1941, the date of the German invasion of Yugoslavia, the six operational IK-3s proved their worth in the fierce fighting against the Luftwaffe, and the last two surviving aircraft were destroyed by their Yugoslavian crew during the night of April 11/12. At that time, another 25 aircraft were under construction.

---

color plate
Rogozarski IK-3 51st Fighter Group Yugoslavian Air Force - Belgrade 1941

Aircraft:	Rogozarski IK-3
Nation:	Yugoslavia
Manufacturer:	Rogozarski A.D.
Type:	Fighter
Year:	1938
Engine:	Hispano-Suiza (Avia) 12 Ycrs, 12-cylinder V, liquid-cooled, 910 hp
Wingspan:	33 ft 10 in (10.30 m)
Length:	26 ft 4 in (8.00 m)
Height:	10 ft 8 in (3.25 m)
Weight:	5,796 lb (2,630 kg)
Maximum speed:	326 mph (526 km/h) at 17,700 ft (5,400 m)
Ceiling:	31,000 ft (9,400 m)
Range:	490 miles (785 km)
Armament:	1 x 20 mm cannon; 2 machine guns
Crew:	1

Prototype of the Rogozarski IK-3.

ITALY

When Italy entered the war, the *Regia Aeronautica* had a total of 3,296 aircraft at its disposal, distributed in Italy itself, in the Aegean area, and in Libya. This total included 1,796 front-line aircraft: 783 bombers, 594 fighters, 268 observation aircraft, and 151 reconnaissance aircraft. Although powerful from a quantitative point of view, this force's potential was clearly totally inferior from a qualitative one when compared to its adversaries, especially as far as its fighters were concerned. On June 10, 1940, more than half these aircraft were Fiat C.R.42 biplanes which were, without a doubt, among the best of their kind, although totally inadequate compared to the contemporary British Hawker Hurricanes and Supermarine Spitfires and to the American Curtiss Kittyhawks and Warhawks used by the Royal Air Force in the Mediterranean area. Likewise, the most modern fighters of the time, such as the Fiat G.50 and the Macchi M.C.200, were also inadequate and, with only two machine guns, they appeared to be practically unarmed when faced with adversaries provided with 6 to 8 weapons, including cannons. As far as the attack aircraft were concerned, experiences in this sector were a total failure, while the situation in the bomber sector was perhaps slightly better: the Fiat B.R.20 and SIAI Marchetti SM.79 could be considered effective on the whole, although they had little defense and were rather vulnerable.

This situation, which was to last almost the entire first year of the conflict, was the result of programs based on outdated criteria and of a general lack of planning and foresight on the part of the high command. Up to that time, Italian military aviation (established as an independent armed force on March 23, 1923) had virtually been living in the past, conditioned above all by combat experiences (such as the Ethiopian campaign and the Spanish Civil War) carried out in particular circumstances that had provided a false impression of the air force and had hampered its modernization. The latter conflict, especially, gave rise to the conviction that the aircraft that had achieved such success in that theater of war would be equally capable of sustaining the burden of a new world war. Consequently, a series of decisions arising from this very same conviction and concerning military and industrial planning led, on the one hand, to the maintaining of many existing production lines beyond reasonable limits and, on the other, to the strengthening of technical, manufacturing, and operative principles that the next few years would prove to be totally inadequate.

Chronology

1938

January 24/25. Three SIAI Marchetti SM.79Ts (*Transatlantico*) cross from Guidonia to Rio de Janeiro (stopping in Dakar), covering the 6,120 miles (9,850 km) in 24 hours and 22 minutes, at an average speed of 251 mph (404 km/h). On December 4, a similar aircraft fitted with 1,000 hp Piaggio P.XI engines breaks the speed record once more, covering 625 miles (1,000 km) at an average speed of 293.798 mph (472.825 km/h), carrying a load of 4,400 lb (2,000 kg). The three-engine bomber, the most famous Italian aircraft of the war, went into service in February 1937. From October 1936 to June 1943, no fewer than 1,217 came off the assembly lines, a number far superior to the production standards of the Italian aeronautical industry at that time.

May 23. The prototype of the Fiat C.R.42 biplane, the last biplane in the world to be built in any great number (1,781), makes its maiden flight. In May 1939, the aircraft was to go into service in the 53rd air regiment based at Caselle. When Italy entered the war, 272 C.R.42s were operative. June 1940 marked the beginning of a long career that continued without interruption on all fronts right up to the end of the war. In September 1943, only 113 C.R.42s remained, and only 64 of these were in an operative state.

October 22. A Caproni Ca.22 *bis* biplane piloted by Mario Pezzi breaks the world ceiling record, reaching an altitude of 56,194 ft (17,083 m). This record is still unbroken in the propellered aircraft with piston engine category.

1939

January. The first of the production series Fiat G.50s are sent to Spain for a number of operative evaluations; 782 of these fighters (the first with retractable landing gear and of the monoplane type to be produced in Italy) were built, and they went into service toward the end of the year.

May 24. The prototype of the Reggiane Re.2000 takes to the air. In spite of its merits, this modern combat plane did not enjoy much success with the *Regia Aeronautica*. In fact, the aircraft (the last of the first generation fighters) was rejected and subsequently produced for export only.

June. Production of the Macchi M.C.200 *Saetta* (the *Regia Aeronautica*'s best first generation fighter) commences and was to continue up to July 1942, when the 1,151st was completed. The aircraft's prototype had made its maiden flight on December 24, 1937, and 144 planes were operative when the war broke out.

November 24. The first (and only) four-engine Italian bomber to be built during the conflict takes to the air. Although particularly advanced and with an excellent performance, very few Piaggio P.108s were built (only 24), and their operative career was rather limited.

FIAT B.R.20 M

Formation of B.R.20 M bombers flying toward French targets in June 1940.

Together with the SIAI Marchetti SM.79 and the CANT Z.1007 *bis*, the Fiat B.R.20 was the standard bomber of the *Regia Aeronautica* during World War II. Although it was the only two-engine aircraft of the three, as opposed to the three-engine formula that characterized the production of large aircraft in Italy for years, it proved to be equally competitive in terms of overall performance, and more than 500 planes were produced from 1936 to July 1943, and these served on practically all fronts until the armistice.

The prototype of the B.R.20, designed by Celestino Rosatelli and christened *Cicogna* (Stork), took to the air for the first time on February 10, 1936, and immediately made a favorable impression. The aircraft was a cantilever low-wing monoplane with an all-metal airframe and mixed aluminum and canvas covering, a completely retractable landing gear, and it was powered by a pair of 1,000 hp Fiat A.80 RC.41 radial engines that drove three-bladed metal propellers. Defensive armament consisted of three machine guns installed in the front, the belly, and the rear, while the bomb

A Fiat B.R.20 bomber with prewar markings.

Close up detail of nose of a B.R.20. The subsequent variants were modified with more glazing.

load reached 3,527 lb (1,600 kg). As for its performance, this more than fulfilled the official specifications, which called for a maximum speed of 240 mph (385 km/h) and the possibility of carrying 2,640 lb (1,200 kg) of bombs for a range of 600 miles (1,000 km).

Following a series of operational evaluations, the B.R.20 went into production. In the meantime, in the wake of propagandistic encouragement by the Fascist regime, two special versions of the aircraft (B.R.20 A) were prepared, largely modified, to participate in long distance races. They were entered in the prestigious Istres-Damascus-Paris race of 1937, and although they arrived in only sixth and seventh place, they provided ample proof of their speed and long-range accomplishments. Success arrived in 1937, however, in the form of a world record for its category gained by another modified aircraft (the B.R.20 L, christened *Santo Francesco*), piloted by Maner Lualdi, which carried out a non-stop flight from Rome to Addis Abeba on March 6, covering about 2,800 miles (4,500 km) at an average speed of over 250 mph (404 km/h).

However, the civilian achievements of the B.R.20 were few when compared to its military ones. The two-engine aircraft had its baptism of fire in Spain in 1937, part of an operational service that lasted for a year and a half. At the outbreak of World War II, it took part in the earliest campaigns, starting with the one in France. In June 1940, the *Regia Aeronautica* had a total of 216 B.R.20s in service and the initial production series (233 aircraft built up to February, 85 of which had been sold to Japan, where they were renamed Type 1) had already been replaced by a second variant, the B.R.20 M (modifications being mainly of a structural nature), 264 of which would be completed by the spring of 1942. These aircraft took part in the *Regia Aeronautica*'s only combat experience in the Battle of Britain: 80 B.R.20 Ms were incorporated into the Italian Air Corps and sent to Belgium, from where they carried out raids on England from October to December 1940. The experience was not a positive one: in the course of missions totalling fewer than 300 hours in all, 20 or so aircraft were shot down, proving their overall inferiority compared to the British fighters. The remaining aircraft were withdrawn.

The final variant of the *Cicogna* was the 1942 B.R.20 *bis*, of which only 15 were produced in the early months of the following year. The front part of the fuselage was redesigned, and the aircraft was fitted with 1,250 hp Fiat A.82 RC.32 engines. The increase in power improved the plane's performance noticeably and allowed for better armament, although these aircraft never went into service.

color plate
Fiat B.R.20 M 43° Gruppo B.T. Regia Aeronautica (43rd Bombers Group *Regia Aeronautica*) - Battle of Britain Belgium 1941

Aircraft:	Fiat B.R.20
Nation:	Italy
Manufacturer:	Fiat SA
Type:	Bomber
Year:	1937
Engine:	2 Fiat A.80 RC.41,18-cylinder radial, air-cooled, 1,000 hp each
Wingspan:	70 ft 8 in (21.53 m)
Length:	52 ft 10 in (16.10 m)
Height:	14 ft 1 in (4.30 m)
Weight:	21,850 lb (9,900 kg) loaded
Maximum speed:	286 mph (460 km/h) at 16,400 ft (5,000 m)
Ceiling:	29,500 ft (9,000 m)
Range:	1,860 miles (3,000 km)
Armament:	3 machine guns; 3,527 lb (1,600 kg) of bombs
Crew:	5

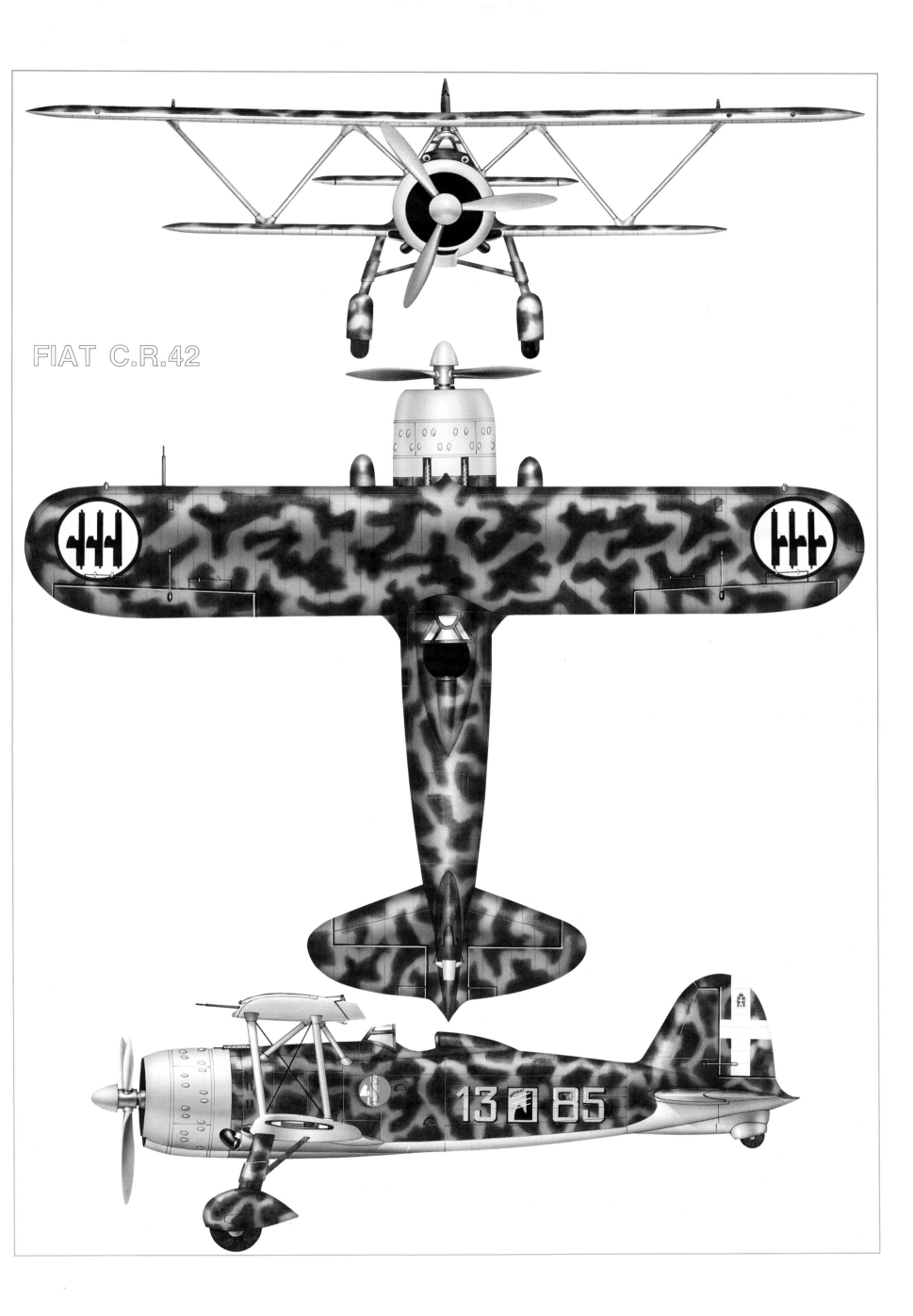

FIAT C.R.42

The Fiat C.R.42 *Falco*, the *Regia Aeronautica*'s last biplane fighter, was paradoxically the combat aircraft built in the greatest number by the Italian aeronautical industry during the conflict. In fact, no fewer than 1,781 of these agile and robust aircraft came off the assembly lines in the course of production, which — despite the presence of (and obvious need for) more modern and competitive planes, such as the Fiat G.50 and the Macchi M.C.200 and 202 — continued uninterruptedly from February 1939 to June 1943.

Created in a period when the monoplane had already gained predominance over the biplane (especially with the excellent aircraft produced by the British and German aeronautical industries), the C.R.42 was the most obvious result of an error of judgment made by the military high command based on combat experiences in the Spanish Civil War. Among the various aircraft that Italy had sent to flank the German Condor Legion was another biplane fighter, the Fiat C.R.32, an extremely agile aircraft that was fast and well armed. Its excellent qualities aroused great enthusiasm both in the technicians and the strategists, and these very experiences gave rise to the conviction that a combat plane should be endowed with such qualities as lightness and maneuverability, considered ideal in close-range confrontations, to the detriment of other characteristics, such as speed, sturdiness, and firepower.

The C.R.42, christened *Falco* (Hawk), was developed following these criteria, with the aim of improving still further the characteristics of its predecessor. Its designer was once again Celestino Rosatelli, the technician who had created the Model 32 in 1933. Rosatelli maintained the overall layout of the earlier aircraft, especially as far as the sesquiplane type wing was concerned, and modified its structure in order to make it more suited to carry a radial engine (considered safer and more reliable) instead of an in-line one. This step was achieved through the production of two experimental models, designated the C.R.40 and the C.R.41 respectively, and the new prototype made its maiden flight on May 23, 1938.

From the beginning, the C.R.42 produced reasonably satisfactory results, and it went into production immediately on the basis of an initial order for 200 aircraft, the first of which came off the assembly lines in February 1939. The plane had an all-metal airframe and a mixed canvas and aluminum covering, as well as fixed, completely faired landing gear. The cockpit was open, and the pilot had good visibility, thanks to the "clean" lines of the wing struts. It was powered by an 840 hp Fiat A.74 RC.38 radial engine, while the armament consisted of two 12.7 mm fixed machine guns mounted in the nose and synchronized to fire through the propeller, which was three-bladed, variable pitch and metal.

In May 1939, the 53rd air regiment based at Caselle became the first Italian unit to be equipped with the new fighter, and when Italy entered the war 272 C.R.42s were in service. June 1940 marked the beginning of a long active career, that continued without interruption on all fronts up to the end of the conflict. By September 1943, only 113 C.R.42s remained, of which 64 were operational. The aircraft was used most of all in the Mediterranean area and, more particularly, in Africa. With the arrival of a new generation of aircraft, the *Falco* was relegated to less demanding roles, such as escort, reconnaissance, ground attack, and night fighter.

The C.R.42 was a successful export aircraft and was ordered by Belgium (40 aircraft), Hungary (68), and Sweden (72).

---

color plate

Fiat. C.R.42 18° Gruppo Caccia Terrestre, 85ª Squadriglia Regia Aeronautica (18th Fighters Group, 85th Squadron *Regia Aeronautica*) - Battle of Britain Belgium 1941

Aircraft:	Fiat C.R.42
Nation:	Italy
Manufacturer:	Fiat SA
Type:	Fighter
Year:	1939
Engine:	Fiat A.74 RC.38, 14-cylinder radial, air-cooled, 840 hp
Wingspan:	31 ft 10 in (9.70 m)
Length:	27 ft 3 in (8.30 m)
Height:	11 ft 9 in (3.58 m)
Weight:	5,060 lb (2,295 kg) loaded
Maximum speed:	272 mph (439 km/h) at 19,700 ft (6,000 m)
Ceiling:	33,550 ft (10,200 m)
Range:	480 miles (775 km)
Armament:	2 machine guns
Crew:	1

Formation of Fiat C.R.42 fighters flying over the Libyan desert in the summer of 1940.

Like the great Messerschmitt Bf.109, its direct adversary, the Supermarine Spitfire gained fame as a fighter par excellence. In the two opposing camps for which they fought, both of these aircraft became the very symbols of the nations in which they had originated. From many points of view, the development of each was conditioned by the existence of the other, by the continuous search for a margin of superiority that would lead to the gaining and maintaining of air supremacy. This confrontation began during the Battle of Britain and continued without interruption throughout World War II.

The Spitfire proved to be an aircraft that was potentially more powerful than its counterpart. This is demonstrated by the fact that, by means of a series of constant improvements, Reginald J. Mitchell's project always remained highly competitive — so much so, in fact, that its final variants remained in front-line service with the RAF well into the 1950s, when the propeller and piston engine had already been superseded by the jet. No fewer than 20,531 Spitfires, in approximately 40 versions, came off the assembly lines — the highest number of any British aircraft. The development of this remarkable series can be appreciated with the help of a few figures: the first prototype had a 990 hp Rolls-Royce Merlin C engine and was capable of reaching a maximum speed of 350 mph (562 km/h); the aircraft belonging to the F.XVIII series were powered by 2,375 hp Rolls-Royce Griffon 67s, while the 1945 Spitfire F.22 could reach a maximum speed of 450 mph (725 km/h). In the course of production, firepower (an element of prime importance in a fighter, since the quality and type of armament adopted had a direct influence on the aircraft's performance) was actually tripled, from 1,800 grams per minute to 5,400 grams.

The origins of the Spitfire provide what may be the clearest indication of the great influence that racing events had on the development of aeronautical technology in the period between the two wars. Its origins can be traced back to the series of racing seaplanes created by Mitchell in the late 1920s for the Schneider Cup, a series that culminated in the Supermarine S.6B,

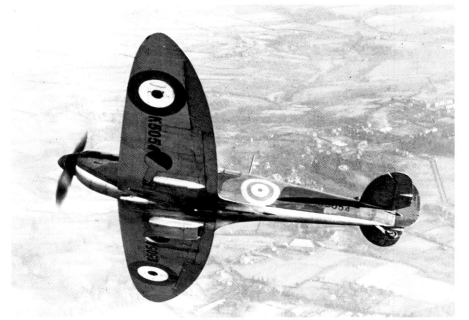

Spitfire Mk.I of the initial production series, with two-bladed wooden propeller.

which won the coveted trophy outright on September 13, 1931, with a speed of 339.82 mph (547.22 km/h). Many of the technical and technological characteristics of these aircraft were adopted once again in the Spitfire, including the power plant developed by Rolls-Royce from the 2,350 hp R type engine that had made victory possible.

The prototype of the Spitfire took to the air for the first time on March 5, 1936. The fighter represented the culmination of a long study phase that had begun in 1934. It was a small, all-metal single-seater with retractable landing gear, and it had carefully studied aerodynamic lines and characteristic, elliptical wings. Moreover, its armament was to be especially powerful, considering that it included eight machine guns.

Flight tests and evaluations exceeded even the most optimistic expectations, and an initial order was placed in June for 310 aircraft. Production began in 1937, with the Mk.I series, and was soon going ahead at a great pace. By October 1939, total orders already amounted to over 4,000 aircraft. Nevertheless, reequipping was relatively slow: the Spitfire Mk.Is (of which 1,583 were built before giving way to the 1940 Mk.II version) went into service in June 1938, and barely nine squadrons were operational when the war broke out. However, this number had increased to 19 in the period immediately prior to the Battle of Britain.

A Spitfire Mk.IB with three-bladed propeller and wing armament consisting of cannons and machine guns.

A Supermarine Spitfire Mk.IIB with cannons on the wings.

color plate

Supermarine Spitfire Mk.I 610th Fighter Squadron (County of Chester) - Battle of Britain England 1941

Aircraft:	Supermarine Spitfire Mk.I
Nation:	Great Britain
Manufacturer:	Supermarine Divison of Vickers-Armstrong Ltd.
Type:	Fighter
Year:	1938
Engine:	Rolls-Royce Merlin II, 12-cylinder V, liquid-cooled, 1,030 hp
Wingspan:	36 ft 10 in (11.22 m)
Length:	29 ft 11 in (9.12 m)
Height:	11 ft 5 in (3.48 m)
Weight:	5,332 lb (2,415 kg) loaded
Maximum speed:	355 mph (571 km/h) at 19,000 ft (5,800 m)
Ceiling:	34,000 (10,360 m)
Range:	500 miles (805 km)
Armament:	8 machine guns
Crew:	1

GREAT BRITAIN

When the war broke out, the only nation in Europe capable of withstanding a confrontation with Germany at an aeronautical level was Great Britain. On October 16, 1939 the aircraft ready for action on British soil numbered 1,500. To these could be added a similar number of reserves. From May, production had reached a monthly rate of 700 aircraft, while from the point of view of quality, the aircraft already in service could generally be considered competitive with those of the Luftwaffe. The development of the war and its spreading to world proportions subsequently demonstrated the vitality of the British military air force, as well as the strength of the tactical and strategical theories upon which its formation was based.

Following a period of relative stagnation during the 1920s and early 1930s, the decisive phase in the strengthening of the Royal Air Force (established as an independent air force on April 1, 1918) had begun in 1933. In that year, the General Staff, putting into practice a series of previsions that would prove to be very timely, invited manufacturers to produce a single-seater fighter with eight machine guns. Then, in 1934, well armed, long-range heavy bombers were commissioned, followed in 1936 by a commission for the first four-engine bombers. These initiatives were based on a careful and solid evaluation of the problems of air warfare, reached by the high command under the guidance of General Hugh Trenchard, one of the RAF's major strategists. In short, while other countries were still discussing the pros and cons of a strong military aviation, Great Britain had already reached the conclusion that the fighter was the most suitable means of defending airspace and that the bomber, in its turn, constituted a fundamental strategic offensive weapon.

In 1937, as a result of these efforts, the RAF (whose main components were Fighter Command, Bomber Command, and Coastal Command) already had the Hurricane, its first modern monoplane fighter, in an operative state and was preparing to put the Spitfire in service. Among the bombers, the most representative aircraft were the twin-engine Blenheim, the Hampden, the Wellington, and the Whitley, some of which were already in service, others about to become operative. The aeronautical industry withstood the sudden increase in pace that was imposed upon it perfectly: in 1938 it succeeded in producing a total of 4,000 aircraft, a number that was to increase to 7,000 in the following year.

However, the strengthening process did not involve only the aircraft themselves and operative organization. The priority given to the need to defend national territory and the almost total certainty that Great Britain would be among the first targets to be attacked by the Germans had led to the creation of a chain of radar stations along the south coast of England from 1935 onward. In July 1939, this network consisted of 20 such stations, capable of sighting aircraft up to 60/125 miles (100/200 km) away at altitudes of over 9,870 ft (3,000 m) and of communicating details of their routes directly to central command. This structure's baptism of fire was to take place during the Battle of Britain, in which it proved to be fundamental in the use of the fighter units to the best advantage against the heavy and incessant German raids.

The modernization of the Fleet Air Arm was much slower, however. It did not become fully independent as an armed force until May 1939. At the outbreak of the war, the aircraft based on board Royal Navy ships (including the six aircraft carriers *Courageous, Furious, Glorious, Eagle, Hermes,* and *Ark Royal*) numbered 225, out of a total of 340. This quantitative lack, worsened by a great qualitative difference compared to the RAF, would improve only during the early years of the conflict.

Chronology

1938

June. The most famous British fighter of the war, the Supermarine Spitfire, goes into service (with the 19th Squadron of the RAF's Fighter Command). From March 1937 to October 1947, 20,531 of these aircraft were produced in approximately 40 versions.

October 11. The prototype fo the Westland Whirlwind heavy fighter, the RAF's first twin-engine single-seater, takes to the air. However, in practice the aircraft did not fulfill expectations.

October 15. The RAF's first twin-engine monoplane torpedo aircraft, the Bristol Beaufort, makes its maiden flight. It went into service in December 1939, and 1,121 were built.

December 12. The prototype of the Fairey Albacore takes to the air. It was destined to replace the Fairey Swordfish in the role of torpedo plane based on board ship. It went into service from 1940, and a total of 800 were built.

1939

March 3. Maiden flight of the prototype of the Wellington Mk.II (which would be followed by the first of the Mk.III series on May 16), one of the most widely used of the first generation British bombers. Between 1937 and 1945, a total of 11,461 were built.

March. The first twin-engine Blenheim Mk.IVs, a strengthened version of the famous medium bomber, are delivered to the units. When the war broke out, 168 of the Mk.IV variant (built toward the end of 1938) were operative. Total production amounted to 3,983 aircraft.

May. Maiden flight of the prototype of the Short Stirling, the RAF's first four-engine bomber; 2,371 were built.

July 17. The prototype of the Bristol Beaufighter, one of the RAF's most potent aircraft, takes to the air. It proved to be an excellent night bomber, torpedo plane, and attack aircraft. Up to September 1945, 5,562 were built.

July 25. The prototype of the twin-engine Avro Manchester bomber takes to the air. The most famous and powerful British bomber, the Lancaster (7,366 of which were built from the end of 1941 up to the early months of 1946), was derived from it.

October 25. The prototype of the four-engine Handley Page Halifax, the RAF's second heavy bomber, takes to the air. It went into service toward the end of 1940, and 6,176 were built.

VICKERS WELLINGTON Mk.I

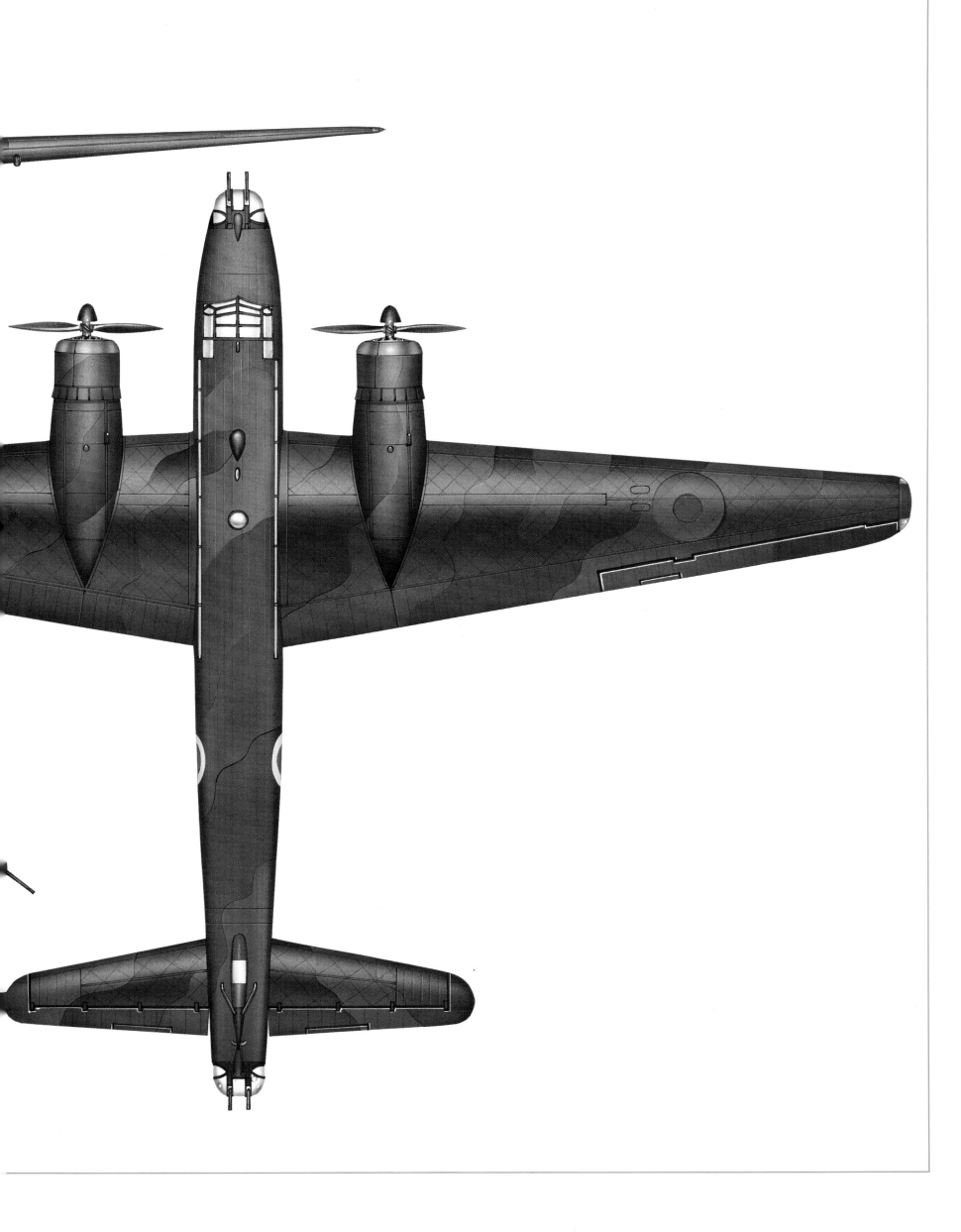

A Vickers Wellington Mk.I of the 214th Squadron in flight before the start of the conflict. The crosses on the insignia are identification marks for use during exercises.

The Wellington was one of the best known and most widely used of the British bombers and, until the appearance of the first heavy bombers, such as the Short Stirling, the Handley Page Halifax, and the Avro Lancaster, it constituted the strong point of the RAF's Bomber Command. In a certain sense, the Wellington was one of the last representatives of a generation of aircraft that characterized military aviation in the 1930s and that were the typical expression of the biplane formula. Although it shared the characteristics of many other models designed in various countries, the Vickers bomber stood out for a technological feature that was to remain unique: its geodetic structure, which combined relative lightness with almost incredible strength. Although it was canvas covered, the Wellington proved capable of standing up to a remarkable amount of punishment and damage while still remaining airborne. Its importance in the RAF's arsenal can be illustrated by a few figures: from 1937 to 1945, 11,461 of this versatile aircraft were built in several versions, serving brilliantly in many roles, from transport to reconnaissance, and in Coastal Command they were used in naval reconnaissance, submarine warfare, and as bombers specialized in mine-laying. Lastly, as a trainer, the Wellington was not withdrawn until 1953.

The prototype made its maiden flight on June 15, 1936, three and a half years after the project had got under way, and a series of flight tests fully confirmed the aircraft's potential. By the end of the year, an order had been placed for 180 planes, and the first Wellington of the initial production series (Mk.I) appeared on December 23, 1937. The two-engine aircraft was immediately christened Wimpey (after a popular cartoon character). It was a mid-wing monoplane with retractable landing gear, powered by a pair of 1,000 hp Bristol Pegasus radial engines and capable of carrying 4,408 lb (2,000 kg) of bombs in its hold. Its defensive

armament was particularly powerful and consisted of six 7.7 mm machine guns installed in two turrets in the nose and the tail and in two lateral positions.

Once production of the first series was complete, other variants soon followed. Among the principal variants, after the Wellington Mk.IA and Mk.IC, which were mainly strengthened in armament (187 Mk.IAs and 2,685 Mk.ICs were built), the prototype of the Mk.II series appeared on March 3, 1939. This was powered by a pair of 1,145 hp Rolls-Royce Merlin X liquid-cooled engines, chosen because of the prospect of the Bristol radials becoming unavailable. On May 16 of the same year, the prototype of the Mk.III series appeared (of which 1,517 were built), marking a return to the use of air-cooled engines with a pair of 1,389 hp Bristol Hercules. Following the Mk.IV (200 of which were built and fitted with Pratt & Whitney Twin Wasp engines), another major production variant was the Mk.X (in fact, the most widely used of all, with 3,803 aircraft being built), fitted with more powerful Bristol Hercules engines.

On the European front, the Wellington's career in the units of Bomber Command came to an end in October 1943. However, it was used extensively in other theaters of war and in the units of Coastal Command, for which variants for naval use had been purposely built. The Mk.VIII series (of which 397 were built) specialized in reconnaissance. This was followed by the Wellington Mk.XI series (numbering 180 aircraft) and the Mk.XII (58), Mk.XIII (844), and Mk.XIV (841) series. The latter aircraft, differing mainly in their engines and armament, were used in a great variety of roles. The final production series (Mk.XV and Mk.XVI), however, were altered as compared to the initial variants and destined for transport: the main modifications consisted in their carrying no armament and in the transformation of the bomb compartment into a hold. The last Wellington, a Mk.X, came off the assembly lines in October 1945.

color plate
Vickers Wellington Mk.I 115th Squadron RAF - Great Britain 1940

A Wellington Mk.II during refuelling prior to a mission in North Africa.

Aircraft:	Vickers Wellington Mk.III
Nation:	Great Britain
Manufacturer:	Vickers-Armstrong Ltd.
Type:	Bomber
Year:	1939
Engine:	2 Bristol Hercules XI, 14-cylinder radial, air-cooled, 1,389 hp each
Wingspan:	86 ft 4 in (26.26 m)
Length:	60 ft 11 in (18.54 m)
Height:	17 ft 5 in (5.31 m)
Takeoff weight:	29,538 lb (13,381 kg)
Maximum speed:	254 mph (410 km/h) at 12,530 ft (3,810 m)
Ceiling:	19,050 ft (5,790 m)
Range:	1,539 miles (2,478 km)
Armament:	8 machine guns; 4,408 lb (2,000 kg) of bombs
Crew:	6

A Vickers Wellington modified with electronic equipment for training.

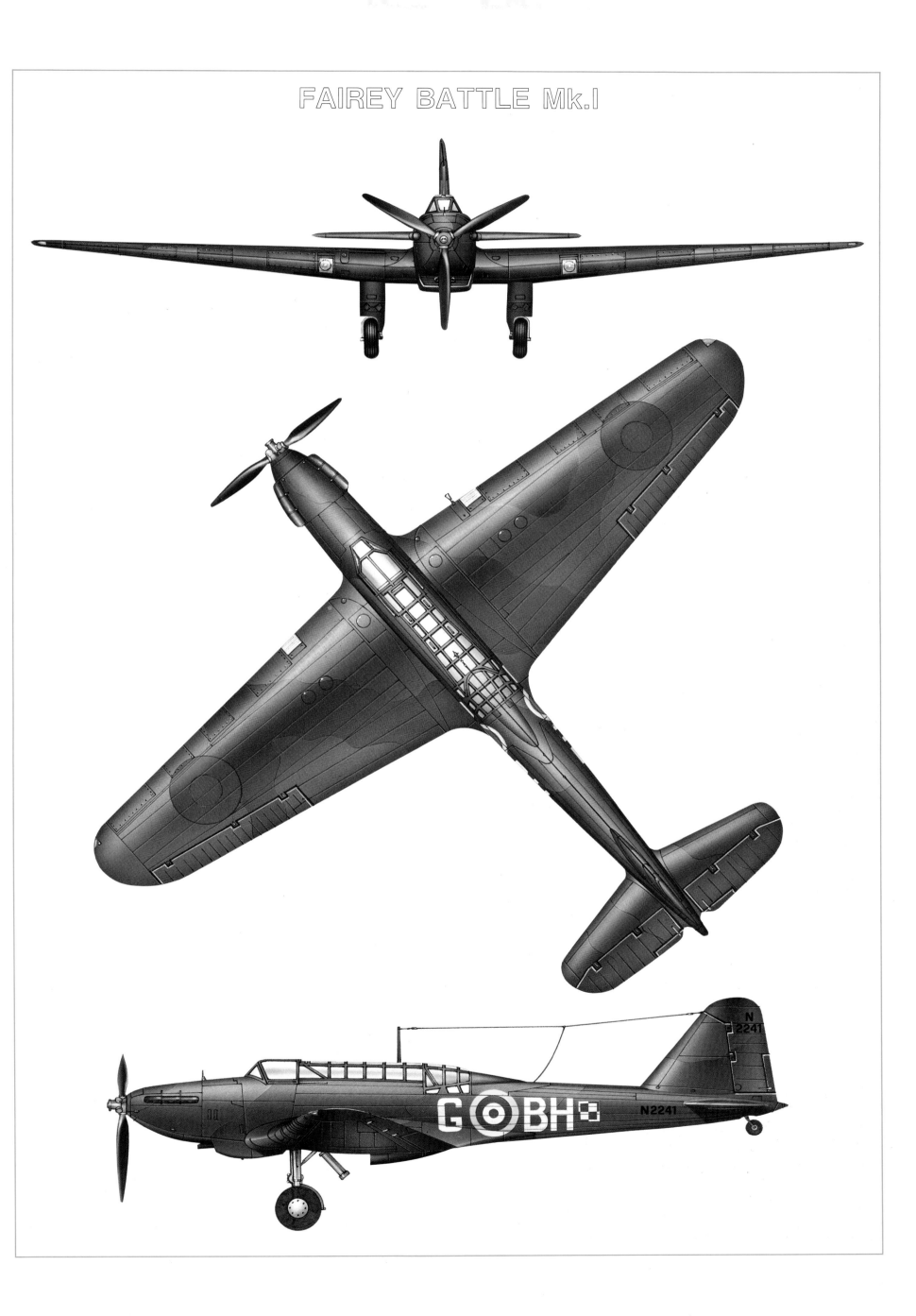

The Fairey Battle was designed in 1933 to replace the biplane light bombers that were still in service in the RAF at the time. It was clearly a transitional aircraft and, as such, proved to be unsuited to the new, more aggressive roles imposed by World War II. Although modern in concept, with an all-metal airframe and retractable landing gear, the Fairey was already out-of-date by the time the war began, and its front-line career lasted approximately a year, up to September 1940. In fact, this date marked the end of production (amounting to 2,185 aircraft out of total orders for 2,419) and virtually coincided with the beginning of the aircraft's withdrawal from front-line duty and its being assigned to less demanding roles, such as training and target towing. Nevertheless, the Fairey bomber was widely used, especially during the early months of the war and especially in the Battle of France, during which it suffered heavy losses.

The prototype of the Battle took to the air for the first time on March 10, 1936. The aircraft had been designed in response to Air Ministry specifications issued in April 1933, calling for a single-engine two-seater bomber capable of carrying a bomb load of 1,000 lb (454 kg) over a distance of 1,050 miles (1,690 km) at a speed of 200 mph (322 km/h). The prototype more than fulfilled these requirements, and, following a series of flight tests and official evaluations, it was accepted by the RAF. It then went into production on the basis of a series of orders amounting to no fewer than 655 aircraft. This number soon increased, so much so that the participation of other manufacturers in the production program became necessary.

The Fairey Battle was a large, low-wing, single-engine aircraft. Its three-man crew (pilot, gunner and radio operator) was housed in a large, completely glazed cockpit; the bomb load was completely contained inside the wings, while the defensive armament consisted of a fixed machine gun in a half-wing and another flexible one in the rear. The aircraft was powered by an engine that was to become famous, the Rolls-Royce Merlin Mk.I generating 1,030 hp and driving a three-bladed, variable pitch metal propeller.

The first Battle Mk.I was delivered to an operative unit in March 1937, and by the end of the year 85 aircraft had been completed. However, by the time the war broke out, this figure had increased and amounted to more than 1,000 (the production series differed above all in the adoption of successive versions of the Merlin engine).

The Fairey bombers had the honor of carrying out the first missions of the war and, having been sent to France on September 2, 1939, as part of the British Advanced Air Striking Force, one of these aircraft shot down the first German aircraft of the conflict, on September 20. On this occasion, however, the aircraft's limitations became apparent, especially its inability to defend itself when attacked by enemy fighters. Although the Battles were therefore withdrawn from daylight operations, the developments of the war soon caused this decision to be changed and, in the spring of 1940, the aircraft were sent, almost at their own risk, to oppose the German advance. The most tragic date was May 14, 1940, during an attack on bridges and a concentration of troops at Sedan, when 40 of the 71 Battles taking part were shot down. During the next few weeks, the units were recalled to Great Britain, and the gradual withdrawal of the bomber from front-line duty began.

Within the context of Commonwealth training programs, many Battles were sent to Australia and Canada. The Royal Australian Air Force used 364, and the Royal Canadian Air Force no fewer than 739.

color plate
Fairey Battle Mk.I 300th (Masovian) Polish Squadron RAF - 1940

Aircraft:	Fairey Battle
Nation:	Great Britain
Manufacturer:	Fairey Aviation Co. Ltd.
Type:	Bomber
Year:	1937
Engine:	Rolls-Royce Merlin Mk.I, 12-cylinder V, liquid-cooled, 1,030 hp
Wingspan:	54 ft (16.46 m)
Length:	52 ft 1 in (15.87 m)
Height:	15 ft 6 in (4.72 m)
Weight:	10,792 lb (4,895 kg) loaded
Maximum speed:	241 mph (388 km/h) at 13,000 ft (3,960 m)
Ceiling:	23,500 ft (7,160 m)
Range:	1,050 miles (1,690 km)
Armament:	2 machine guns; 1,000 lb (454 kg) of bombs
Crew:	3

A Fairey Battle serving in the British Advanced Air Striking Force, stationed in France in September 1939.

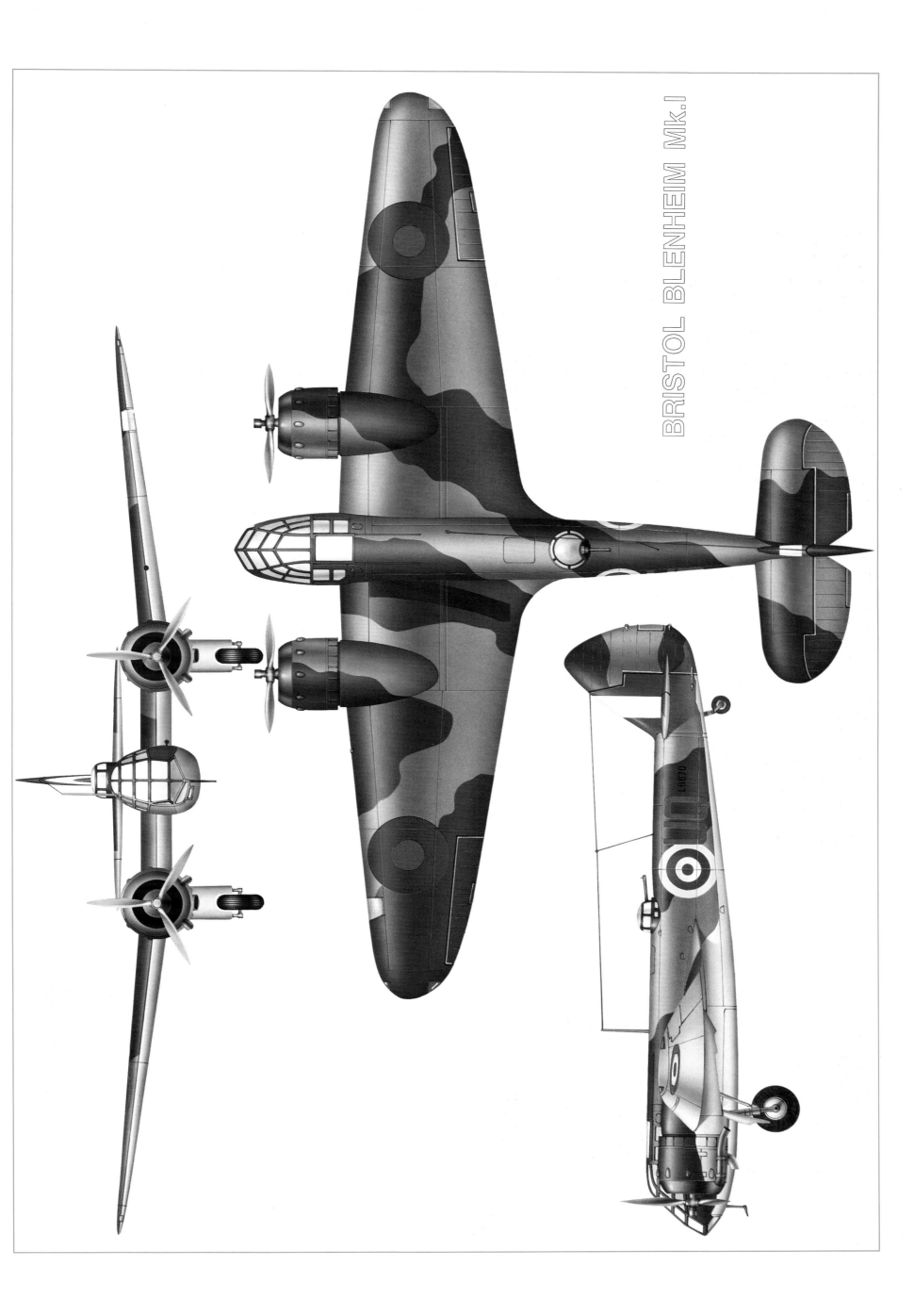

BRISTOL BLENHEIM Mk.I

A Blenheim Mk.I at Addis Abeba airport in front of *Ala Littoria*'s destroyed air terminal.

A Blenheim Mk.I of the 211th Squadron ready for takeoff from a Greek airport in 1941.

generating 608 hp) in the airframe then in construction and, in this configuration, the prototype (designated Type 142) made its maiden flight on April 12, 1935. It was an elegant all-metal, low-wing aircraft, with retractable landing gear. It was particularly impressive as far as speed was concerned: during flight tests it reached almost 307 mph (495 km/h), a performance superior to that of any other British fighter at the time.

Two months later, impressed by the aircraft's remarkable qualities, Lord Rothermere presented it to the nation. The Air Ministry lost no time in evaluating the transformation of the prototype into a bomber and, in September, placed an initial order for 150 production series aircraft. However, adapting the aircraft for military use did not prove to be a simple task. The Blenheim had to be substantially modified, especially the wing structure (the wings were, in fact, raised to provide bomb housing) and the fuselage, in order to provide positions for the armament.

The first prototype of the series took to the air on June 25, 1936, and deliveries of the aircraft to the units commenced in January 1937. Production was soon going ahead at a great pace and, before passing to the subsequent major production variant, the Mk.IV (built toward the end of 1938), no fewer than 1,552 Blenheim Mk.Is came off the assembly lines. In the new version the designers had taken the operative experiences of the aircraft into account, for these had revealed a certain inadequacy. In fact, as well as being provided with additional armament, the machine guns being increased to five and the bomb load reaching 1,325 lb (600 kg), and more powerful engines (920 hp Bristol Mercury XVs), the Blenheim Mk.IVs also featured modifications to the fuselage (with a different nose structure) and to the wings (containing larger fuel tanks). The first units began to receive the new variant in March 1939, and 168 Blenheim Mk.IVs were operative when the war broke out. Production continued until a total of 3,983 had been completed, including those of a version (Type 149) rejected by the RAF but used by Canada, where they were built on license under the name of Bolingbroke (similar overall to the Blenheim Mk.I but powered by different engines), and 945 Mk.Vs (Type 160), modified above all in their armament and fuselage. However, the latter aircraft never proved to be particularly effective.

Among the minor variants, mention should be made of 200 or so aircraft (Mk.IF) that were converted into heavy fighters and provided with four forward machine guns.

On September 3, 1939, the RAF carried out its first operative mission of World War II (a reconnaissance flight over Germany). The protagonist of this historical event was a small and fast medium bomber, the Bristol Blenheim, and, although not an outstanding combat plane, it proved to be indispensable in its role during the first three years of the war. More than 5,500 Blenheims were built in two major production versions, and they fought on almost all fronts, also bearing the insignia of the Canadian and South African air forces.

The origins of the twin-engine Bristol still constitute an original part of British aviation history. In fact, the Blenheim came into being in 1934, on the initiative of a newspaper magnate, Lord Rothermere, owner of the *Daily Mail,* who asked manufacturers to design a fast, modern twin-engine private transport plane, capable of carrying six passengers and two crew members. Lord Rothermere was very explicit in his request: the aircraft was to be "the fastest commercial plane in Europe, if not the world."

This proposal attracted the attention of the Bristol company, which happened to be working on studies for an aircraft of this type at the time. Frank Barnwell, the designer, had no hesitation in installing two powerful Bristol Mercury radial engines (each

color plate

Bristol Blenheim Mk.I 211th Squadron RAF - Greece 1940

Aircraft:	Bristol Blenheim Mk.I
Nation:	Great Britain
Manufacturer:	Bristol Aeroplane Co. Ltd.
Type:	Bomber
Year:	1937
Engine:	2 Bristol Mercury VIII, 9-cylinder radial, air-cooled, 840 hp each
Wingspan:	56 ft 4 in (17.17 m)
Length:	39 ft 9 in (12.12 m)
Height:	9 ft 10 in (2.99 m)
Weight:	12,500 lb (5,670 kg) loaded
Maximum speed:	260 mph (418 km/h) at 11,800 ft (3,600 m)
Ceiling:	27,280 ft (8,315 m)
Range:	1,215 miles (1,810 km)
Armament:	2 machine guns; 1,000 lb (454 kg) of bombs
Crew:	3

THE UNITED STATES OF AMERICA

On September 1, 1939, date of the German invasion of Poland, the U.S. Army Air Corps (USAAC) had 2,400 aircraft of all types at its disposal, 800 of which were front-line. A further 2,500 aircraft were in service with the U.S. Navy, and 600 of these were based on board ship. In spite of these numbers, it was not a particularly formidable air force: the standard bomber, notwithstanding the presence of 20 or so Boeing B-17s, was still the old twin-engine Douglas B-18; the fighters in service consisted mainly of Northrop A-17s and Curtiss P-36 Hawks, both transitional aircraft. In naval aviation, biplanes, such as the Grumann F3F and the Curtiss SBC Helldiver, still existed next to the first Northrop BT and Douglas TBD Devastator monoplanes.

The general inadequacy that characterized American military aviation when the war broke out in Europe was the result of a series of political, strategical, industrial and economic factors that had marked its evolution during the years of peace, leading it along a path entirely its own. Conditioned by the delays accumulated during the Great War, the process of reorganizing and expanding the air force had continued at an unsteady pace throughout the 1920s and for much of the following decade. It had been a long and complex process, in which moments of great vitality alternated with periods of relative stagnancy, the last of which lasted virtually up to the eve of World War II. Paradoxically during this period considering the almost incredible growth in commercial aviation, military aviation appeared to be relatively little developed and was provided with means that were clearly unsuitable for the new war that was by now looming on the horizon. Behind all this lay the conviction that the United States would be affected only indirectly by the conflict, and even then only from a defensive point of view.

At an organizational level, after the uncertainties of the period immediately following World War I, it was not until July 2, 1926, that the U.S. Army Air Corps (USAAC) was created, and only then had an initial reequipping and strengthening plan been launched. The program, however, went ahead very slowly, conditioned by the political and economic situation of the time and characterized by the strong rivalry between the army aviation and that of the navy. This delayed expansion still further and hampered homogeneity between the two armed forces.

Unlike the USAAC, the Naval Flying Corps had maintained a reasonably effective structure, and its development had been accentuated by the creation (on August 10, 1921), within the Navy Department, of a Bureau of Aeronautics, a group responsible for everything concerning naval aviation. This close tie had directly linked the development of the air force to programs regarding the expansion and strengthening of the fleet. The army, in its turn, did not succeed in creating a single command for the USAAC until March 1, 1935. The final reorganization process took place in June 1941, once the war was already at an advanced stage, when the USAAC was provided with an autonomous General Staff, given semiautonomous status and redesignated the U.S. Army Air Force (USAAF).

The aeronautical industry had also been affected by the situation and, in the absence of a precise stimulus, worked at a reduced rate compared to its enormous potential: in 1938, 1,800 combat aircraft were built, a total that was to increase only marginally the following year (2,195).

The first signs of a revival, both at a qualitative and quantitative level, appeared in 1939, although the efforts were mainly oriented abroad. In fact, the impetus was provided above all by the massive requests coming from France and Great Britain, the first of the Allies to experience the violence of the new conflict at their own expense.

Chronology

1938

April 6. The prototype of the Bell XP-39 Airacobra, one of the most original fighters of the war, makes its maiden flight; 9,588 of these aircraft were built. In the same month, the Northrop BT-1 dive-bomber, the direct predecessor of the Douglas SBD Dauntless, goes into service on the aircraft carrier *Yorktown*.

April 20. Delivery of the first Curtiss P-36A fighters. Together with the Seversky P-35, the P-36 marked the definitive passage from biplane to monoplane in American military aviation. However, both were transitional aircraft and met with limited success in the United States, eventually being produced mainly for export.

October 14. The prototype of the Curtiss P-40, derived from the P-36A, takes to the air. Although not a particularly outstanding fighter, a great number were built and exported to all the Allied countries: from 1939 to 1944, no fewer than 13,733 aircraft, in dozens of versions, came off the assembly lines.

October 26. The prototype of the Douglas Model 78, one of the most widely used twin-engine bomber and attack aircraft of the entire war, makes its maiden flight. It was to become known as DB-7, A-20 and P-70 and in Great Britain by the names Boston and Havoc; 7,385 were built in all.

December 31. The Boeing Model 307 Stratoliner, the world's first pressurized aircraft, makes its maiden flight. This four-engine aircraft was derived from the B-17 bomber and retained its wings, empennage, and engines. During the war, it was requisitioned by the military aviation and redesignated C-75.

1939

January. The prototype of the North American NA-40 takes to the air. After a series of modifications, it was accepted as the B-25 Mitchell. This excellent twin-engine bomber proved to be one of the most versatile and efficient aircraft in its class, and a total of more than 11,000 were built.

January 27. The prototype of the Lockheed XP-38 makes its first flight. The fighter, characterized by its twin-engines and double tail beams, was one of the best of its kind, and 9,923 were built in numerous versions.

February 12. The prototype of the XF4F-3 Wildcat takes to the air. Approximately 8,000 Wildcats were built.

December 29. The prototype of the Consolidated B-24 Liberator, the United States' second most important bomber of the war, takes to the air. Although less famous than the Boeing B-17, no fewer than 18,188 of these four-engine aircraft were built, more than any other similar American plane.

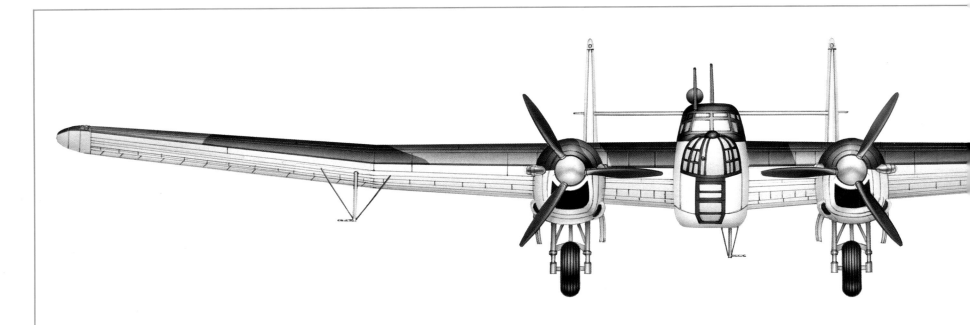

ARMSTRONG WHITWORTH WHITLEY Mk.VII

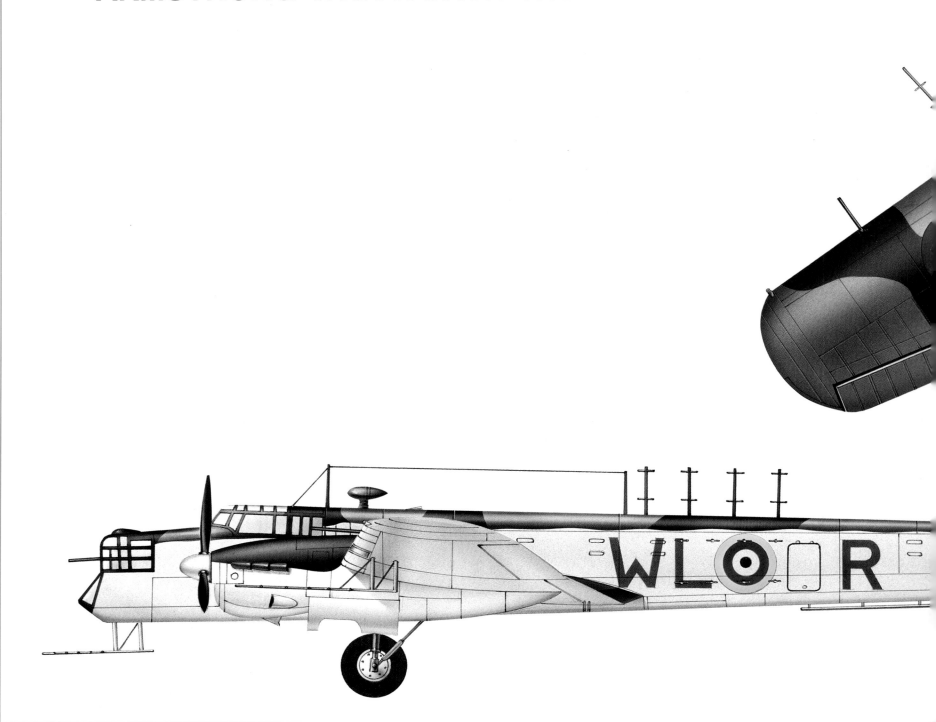

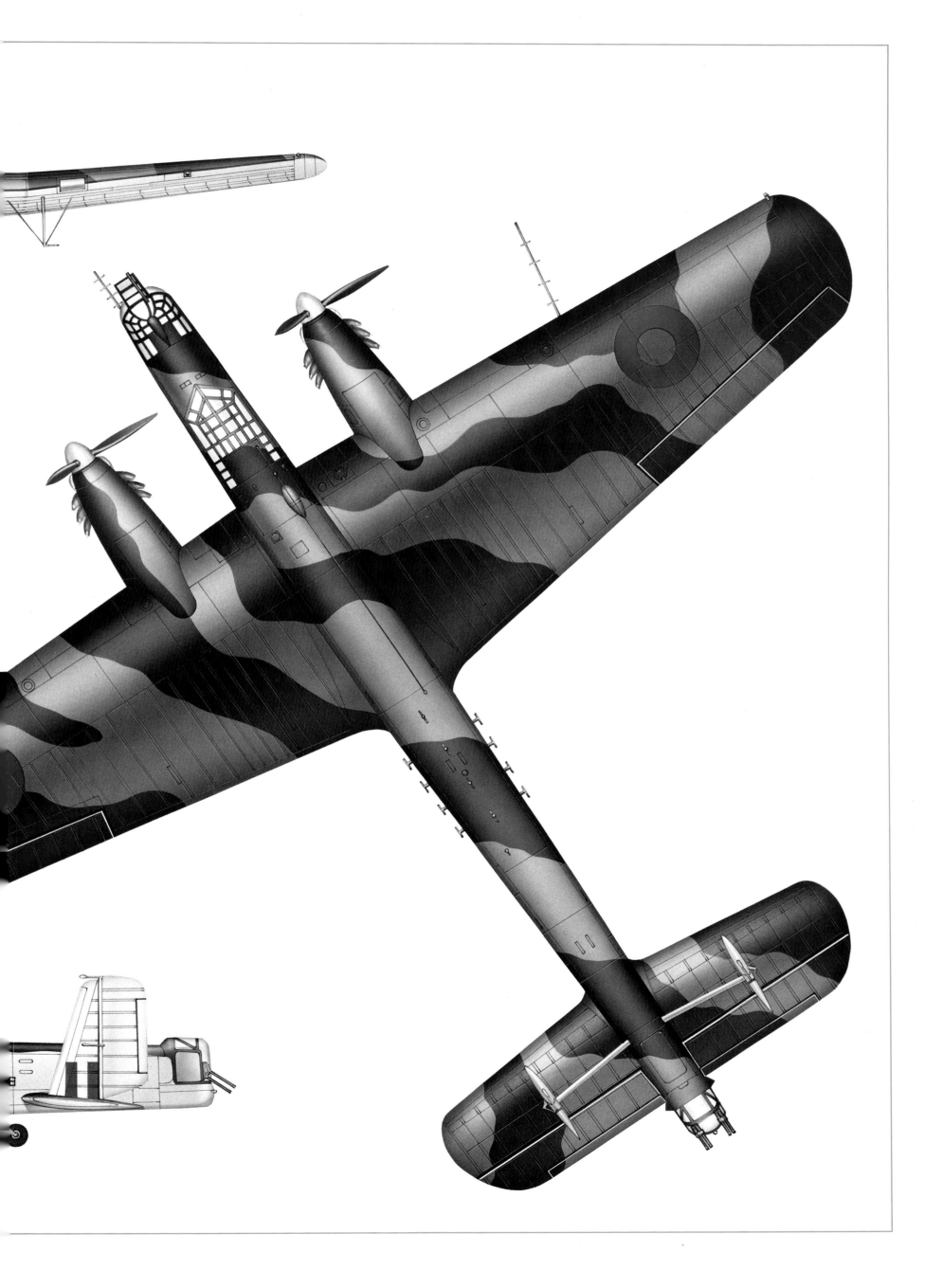

One of the oldest medium bombers in service in the units of the RAF when the war broke out, the Armstrong Whitworth Whitley was clearly a transitional aircraft, the first of the trio of planes of this type (which included the Vickers Wellington and the Handley Page Hampden) built in Great Britain in the period immediately prior to the war. Although outdated by the time the war broke out, and therefore relegated to night missions, the Whitley nevertheless had a long and extensive operative career, considering that a total of 1,814 were built. They remained in front-line service with the units of Bomber Command until the spring of 1942, while those in Coastal Command were withdrawn almost a year later. They were subsequently relegated to secondary roles.

The Whitley originated on the basis of official specifications issued in July 1934, and an initial production order (for 80 aircraft) was placed before the prototype even took to the air. This made its maiden flight on March 17, 1936, powered by a pair of 795 hp Armstrong Siddeley Tiger X radial engines that drove three-bladed, variable pitch metal propellers. It was a large, middle-wing, twin-engine aircraft, with retractable landing gear and vertical twin rudders, in which the most characteristic feature was the wing. This was quite thick, with a large surface area, and was installed in the fuselage at a sharp angle of incidence, which was transformed into a characteristic "nose down" attitude during flight.

Operative tests and evaluations were completed in the fall, and the first Mk.I series aircraft were delivered at the beginning of 1937. However, only very few (34 in all) of these aircraft were built, and they ceded their place on the assembly lines to 46 Whitley Mk.IIs and 80 Mk.IIIs. The difference between these production variants lay mainly in the armament and in the power of the engines (795 hp and 920 hp Tigers, respectively).

In the following version, the Mk.IV (which made its maiden flight on April 5, 1939, and 40 of which were built), the power plants were radically changed, and a pair of 1,030 hp Rolls-Royce Merlin V-12, were fitted, while the defensive armament was strengthened still further, thanks to the installation of a four-machine-gun tail turret. From this series the major production variant (the Mk.V, of which 1,466 were built) was then derived, featuring the installation of more powerful Merlin engines, as well as modifications to the tail fins and the fuselage. The fuel capacity was also increased, thus providing the aircraft with a greater range. Deliveries of the Whitley Mk.V began in 1939 and terminated in the summer of 1943.

The final variant was the Mk.VII, built expressly for Coastal Command and for the role of naval bomber and antisubmarine fighter. Although the 1,145 hp Merlin engines of the Whitley Mk.Vs were retained, the weight of these aircraft increased notably, considering that they were provided with extra tanks, increasing their fuel capacity from 1,005 USgal (3,805 liters) to 1,320 USgal (5,000 liters) and providing them with a range of 1,676 miles (2,700 km). This resulted in an overall reduction in performance, especially as far as speed was concerned. Nevertheless, the Whitley Mk.VIIs proved to be particularly suited to their role: they went into service toward the end of 1941, and were the first Coastal Command bombers to be provided with long-range submarine tracking radar equipment.

The Whitleys took part in all the major combat operations during the early years of the war. Moreover, they were the first British bombers to fly over Berlin (on October 1, 1939, although only to drop leaflets) and the first to drop bombs on Italian territory, over Turin and Genoa, on June 11, 1940.

color plate
Armstrong Whitworth Whitley Mk.VII 612th Squadron Coastal Command Royal Air Force - 1941

Aircraft:	Armstrong Whitworth Whitley Mk.VII
Nation:	Great Britain
Manufacturer:	Armstrong Whitworth Aircraft Ltd.
Type:	Bomber
Year:	1941
Engine:	2 Rolls-Royce Merlin X, 12-cylinder V, liquid-cooled, 1,145 hp each
Wingspan:	84 ft (25.60 m)
Length:	70 ft 6 in (21.49 m)
Height:	15 ft (4.57 m)
Weight:	28,200 lb (12,792 kg) loaded
Takeoff weight:	34,190 lb (15,488 kg)
Maximum speed:	215 mph (346 km/h) at 14,795 ft (4,498 m)
Ceiling:	17,600 ft (5,365 m)
Range:	1,676 miles (2,700 km)
Armament:	5 machine guns; 6,000 lb (2,718 kg) of bombs
Crew:	5/6

An Armstrong Whitworth Whitley. On October 1, 1939, bombers of this type carried out the first daylight raid on Berlin.

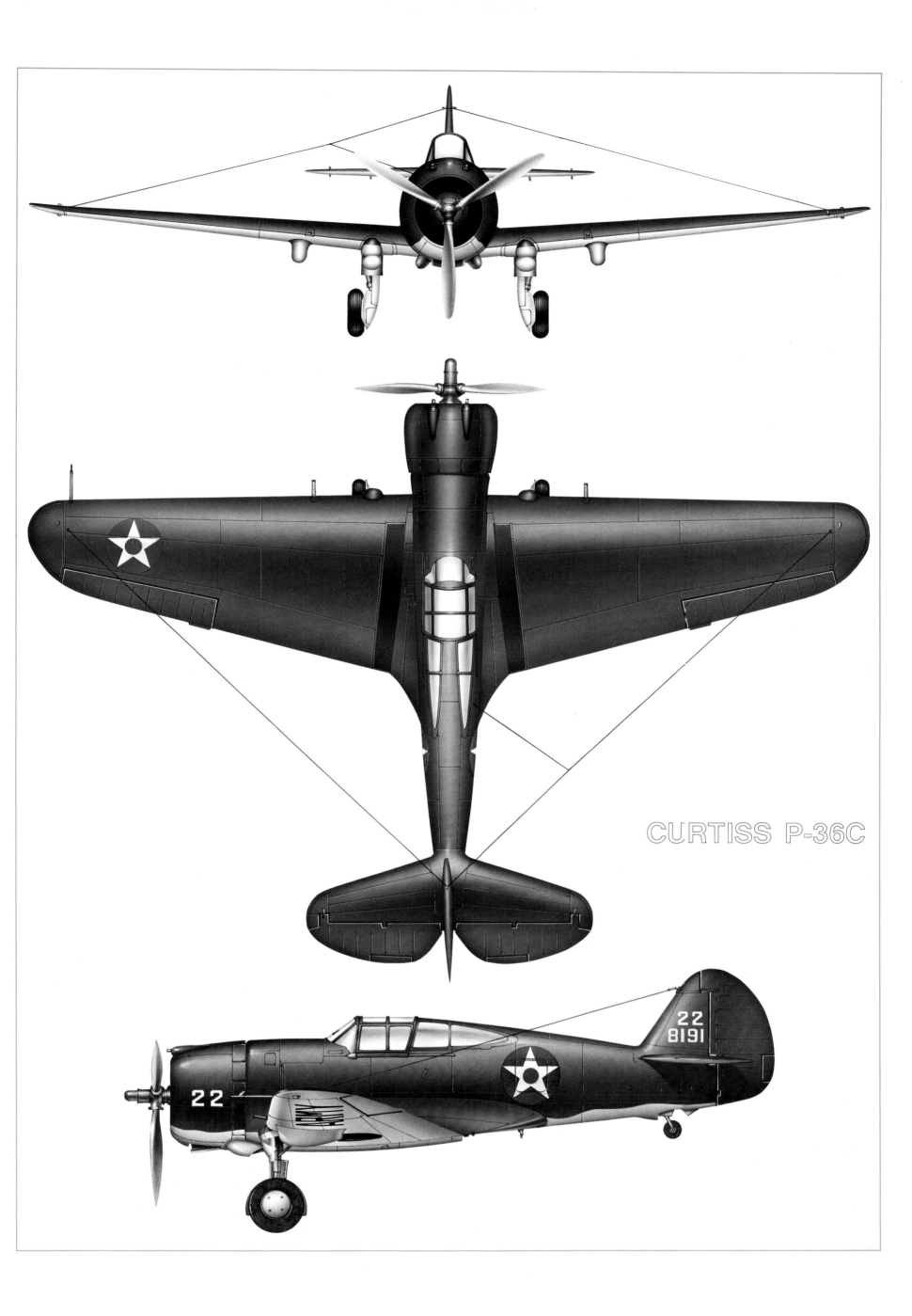

CURTISS P-36C

22
8191

22

The definitive passage from biplane to monoplane in the American military aviation was marked toward the mid-1930s by two fighters: the Curtiss P-36 and the Seversky P-35. However, they were both transitional aircraft that met with only limited success in the United States, eventually being produced mainly for export. In particular, only 210 Curtiss P-36s were delivered to the units, although it remained the USAAC's standard fighter from 1938 until the United States entered the war, and the aircraft concluded its brief operative career at Pearl Harbor on December 7, 1941. During the Japanese attack, most of the 39 P-36As in the base were destroyed on the ground, although four of them managed to take to the air and to shoot down two enemy aircraft.

The project for the Model 75 (the designation given by Curtiss to its new model) was launched in the summer of 1934 by Donovan A. Berlin, an ex-Northrop technician who had just started to work for the old established Buffalo-based manufacturer. The aim was to participate in the competition announced by the USAAC for the construction of a new monoplane fighter with a speed of around 300 mph (483 km/h) to replace the Boeing P-26s that were in their final production phase at the time. Construction work on the prototype commenced on November 1, 1934, and its maiden flight took place on May 15 the following year.

The aircraft was an all-metal, low cantilever wing monoplane, with enclosed cockpit and retractable landing gear, originally powered by a 900 hp Wright XR-1760 radial engine. In the meantime, however, the date of the competition was postponed and it was not until April 10, 1939, that a second Curtiss prototype (with modified power plant) could be evaluated. The results were not exceptional, although the aircraft's potential was recognized in the form of an order for three experimental planes, placed on August 5. In 1937, the USAAC made its choice, with a request for 210 P-36As. The first of the 178 aircraft actually completed was delivered on April 20, 1938, and from December production was concentrated on 32 of the second version, the P-36C, with more powerful engine and armament.

The Curtiss fighter met with greater success on the foreign market. The first sales took place in 1938 and involved a simplified version with fixed landing gear (Model 75H) ordered by Nationalist China (30 aircraft, plus 82 on license), by Thailand (12), and by Argentina (29, plus 200 on license). In 1939, export of the major variant was authorized, and this was built in nine versions (designated H75A-1 to H75A-9), of which the first four were for France and the remaining five, respectively, for China (a single prototype), Norway (24 H75A-6s and 36 H75A-8s ordered), the Netherlands (20 H75A-7s ordered), and Iran (10 H75A-9s ordered, subsequently sent to Great Britain).

However, the greatest user of all was France, which in the effort of rearming just before the war, eventually ordered around 1,000 of these fighters from May 13, 1938, up to October 1939. In practice, however, by June 1940, the *Armée de l'Air* had succeeded in putting only 291 H75As into service, and these fought valiantly to oppose the German invasion. In particular, the Curtiss fighter had the honor of gaining the first French air victory of the conflict. This occurred on September 8, 1939, during combat between five H75A-1s and a squadron of Messerschmitt Bf.109Es, in the course of which two German aircraft were shot down.

The aircraft that had not been delivered to France following the armistice and those that had managed to escape to Britain in the meantime, a total of 227 in all, were incorporated into the Royal Air Force and redesignated Mohawk. However, they were not used on the European front.

---

color plate

Curtiss P-36C Fighting Training Units - United States 1941

Curtiss P-36 Hawk during evaluation tests by the U.S. Army Air Corps.

Prototype of the Curtiss P-36.

Curtiss P-36 of the 51st Pursuit Group with olive markings.

Aircraft:	Curtiss P-36C
Nation:	USA
Manufacturer:	Curtiss Wright Corp.
Type:	Fighter
Year:	1939
Engine:	Pratt & Whitney R-1830-17 Twin Wasp, 14-cylinder radial, air-cooled, 1,200 hp
Wingspan:	37 ft 4 in (11.35 m)
Length:	28 ft 6 in (8.68 m)
Height:	9 ft 4 in (2.84 m)
Weight:	6,150 lb (2,790 kg) loaded
Maximum speed:	311 mph (501 km/h) at 10,000 ft (3,048 m)
Ceiling:	33,700 ft (10,272 m)
Range:	820 miles (1,320 km)
Armament:	2 machine guns
Crew:	1

DOUGLAS TBD-1

0322 TBD-1
US NAVY
6-T-1

DOUGLAS TBD-1

The Douglas TBD Devastator was the first all-metal low-wing monoplane with retractable landing gear to go into service in the U.S. Navy. However, although advanced at the time that occurred, this sturdy and reliable torpedo plane was virtually out-of-date when the war broke out and it found itself fighting with a clear disadvantage compared to the fierce fighters of the enemy. Proof of its being obsolete was dramatically provided on June 4, 1942, during the Battle of Midway: 15 TBD-1s that had taken off from the aircraft carrier *Hornet* to attack the Japanese naval force were literally wiped out (only one managed to return to the carrier) by antiaircraft fire and by the violent counterattack of the Mitsubishi A6M Zeros, against which they were practically defenseless. During the next two days of battle, the fate of the entire torpedo plane force on the carriers *Yorktown*, *Enterprise*, and *Hornet* was sealed, and it was reduced from a total of 41 aircraft to five. This episode in the air-sea battle in the Pacific also marked the end of the Devastator's operative career, which had commenced in November 1937 on board the aircraft carrier *Saratoga*. The total number of aircraft produced was not very high: 129 planes of a single production series version, designated TBD-1.

The project originated in 1934, on the basis of specifications issued by the U.S. Navy calling on manufacturers to design a new carrier-based torpedo plane to operate from the aircraft carriers then being built. As well as Douglas, several other companies participated: prototypes were also prepared by the Great Lakes Aircraft Corporation of Cleveland (XTBG-1, a biplane) and by the Hall Aluminum Aircraft Corporation of Bristol, Pennsylvania (XPTBH-2, a high-wing seaplane). Among the competitors, the XTBD-1 submitted by Douglas clearly appeared the most potent and technologically advanced. It was a low-wing monoplane (the cantilever wings could be folded back by means of hydraulic controls), with all-metal airframe and covering (apart from the rudder and the elevator, which were fabric covered). The main landing gear was partially retractable (the wheels protruding half-way, to facilitate emergency landing). The prototype was powered by an 811 hp Pratt & Whitney XR-1830-60 radial engine, and the three-man crew was housed in a single enclosed cockpit. The aircraft's defensive armament was to consist of two machine guns, one fixed forward one, and another flexible one for the defense of the side and rear sections, and of a 1,000 lb (454 kg) bomb load or a torpedo.

The prototype took to the air for the first time on April 15, 1935, and it began a series of flight tests and operative evaluations at the Anacostia naval base immediately after. This phase proved to be particularly long, and several modifications were carried out, the principal ones being the substitution of the engine, the installation of a better and more aerodynamic engine cowling, and the redesigning of the crew's cockpit. The latter was provided with a different hood, carefully studied to improve the pilot's visibility during landing on deck. The first contract was signed in February 1936, and production commenced immediately after. Deliveries began on June 25, the following year.

When the United States entered the war, 100 TBD-1s were in service, although only 69 could be considered operative. In addition to the Battle of Midway, this torpedo plane took part in all the air-sea operations involving the United States during the first six months of the war and, in spite of everything, generally produced satisfactory results in the role of a traditional bomber.

---

color plate
Douglas TBD-1 V.T.6 *USS Enterprise* - United States 1940

Aircraft:	Douglas TBD-1
Nation:	USA
Manufacturer:	Douglas Aircraft Co.
Type:	Torpedo-bomber
Year:	1937
Engine:	Pratt & Whitney R-1830-64 Twin Wasp, 14-cylinder radial, air cooled, 900 hp
Wingspan:	50 ft 4 in (15.24 m)
Length:	35 ft (10.67 m)
Height:	15 ft 1 in (4.60 m)
Weight:	10,194 lb (4,624 kg) loaded
Maximum speed:	206 mph (332 km/h) at 8,000 ft (2,440 m)
Ceiling:	19,500 ft (6,000 m)
Range:	716 miles (1,150 km)
Armament:	2 machine guns; 1,000 lb (454 kg) of bombs
Crew:	3

A Devastator TBD-1 of the V.T.6 Squadron, based on the *USS Enterprise*.

JAPAN

While German military strength was being unleashed against Europe, on the other side of the world a second deadly war machine was preparing for action. In 1939, the true extent of Japan's rearmament was still almost unknown in the West, despite the worrying signs emerging from the conflict with China. In the aeronautical field in particular, there was a widespread conviction that the development of military aircraft in Japan had been slower than in the countries traditionally considered to be in the vanguard in this sector. Right up to the eve of the United States entering the war, experts and strategists were still convinced that, on the other side of the Pacific, manufacturers were producing outdated aircraft, copied or derived from foreign ones, and that their technology was totally dependent on that of the principal Western suppliers.

Rarely in the course of history has a conviction proved to be so mistaken. The Japanese attack followed little more than two years after that of Hitler, although it was devastating nevertheless. The strength and advanced nature of the Empire of the Rising Sun's navy and air force, as well as their extreme efficiency, were revealed for the first time on the day of the events at Pearl Harbor. This state of affairs continued through the first six months of war in the Pacific, and the United States was subsequently forced to make a great effort in order to regain supremacy of the air,

faced with an adversary that proved to be increasingly powerful and aggressive.

Throughout the 1930s, the potential of the Japanese aviation had passed almost unnoticed by the rest of the world. More especially, the vast reorganization process in its industrial network had passed unnoticed. This had been under way since the end of World War I and had led to the creation of a massive productive structure that was almost completely oriented toward military production. The army and the navy had played a particularly active role in this phase since, due to the continuous rivalry between them, they competed to build increasingly perfect aircraft that were increasingly suited to warfare. Both forces had concentrated on developing their respective aeronautical components. The Imperial navy's air force was the elder, having been founded in 1912, while the army's had been formally established on May 1, 1925.

Following the experiences of the conflict with China, Japan's preparations for World War II can be clearly illustrated by its aeronautical production figures during the three years immediately preceding the outbreak of the conflict in Europe: the 445 aircraft produced in 1930 increased to 952 in 1935, to 1,181 in 1936, to 1,511 in 1937, to 3,201 in 1938, and to 4,467 in 1939. The increase in production was accompanied by a further strengthening of the industrial network, which became more flexible and competitive.

Chronology

1938

January. The prototype of the Aichi D3A, one of the best dive-bombers of its time, makes its maiden flight. It was the first Japanese aircraft to bomb American targets during the war, as well as the aircraft that succeeded in sinking the greatest number of Allied warships. It remained in production from December 1939 until August 1945, and 1,495 were built in three main versions.

March. Operative debut, in China, of the Nakajima Ki-27, a small and agile fighter that marked the passage from the biplane to aircraft of the next generation in the Imperial army's aviation. From the end of 1937 up to 1942, no fewer than 3,399 were built.

1939

January. The prototype of the Nakajima Ki-43 Hayabusa, the Ki-27's direct successor and the Japanese army's first modern fighter, makes its maiden flight. A total of 5,919 were built and remained in service from the first day of the war to the last.

April 1. The prototype of the Mitsubishi A6M1, which was to become famous under the name Zero, takes to the air. It was the first modern monoplane fighter to be built in Japan, and it went down in history as one of the best of the entire war, becoming the very symbol of the Empire of the Rising Sun's strength in the air. A total of 10,499 of these aircraft came off the assembly lines between March 1939 and August 1945.

August 26. A Mitsubishi G3M2 bomber, converted for civilian use, registered J-BACI and christened *Nippon,* flies round the world, covering over 32,820 miles (52,850 km) in 194 hours of flying time.

October 23. The prototype of the Mitsubishi G4M1, the Imperial navy's most famous and widely used bomber of the entire war, makes its maiden flight; 2,446 of these twin-engine aircraft were built up to August 1945.

November. The prototype of the Mitsubishi Ki-46, the Japanese army's best reconnaissance aircraft, appears. In all, 1,742 were built. This elegant twin-engine aircraft's remarkable performance was demonstrated in February 1945, when two prototypes of the final Ki-46-IV version covered 1,429 miles (2,301 km) at an average speed of 435 mph (700 km/h), although this was with the help of favorable tailwinds.

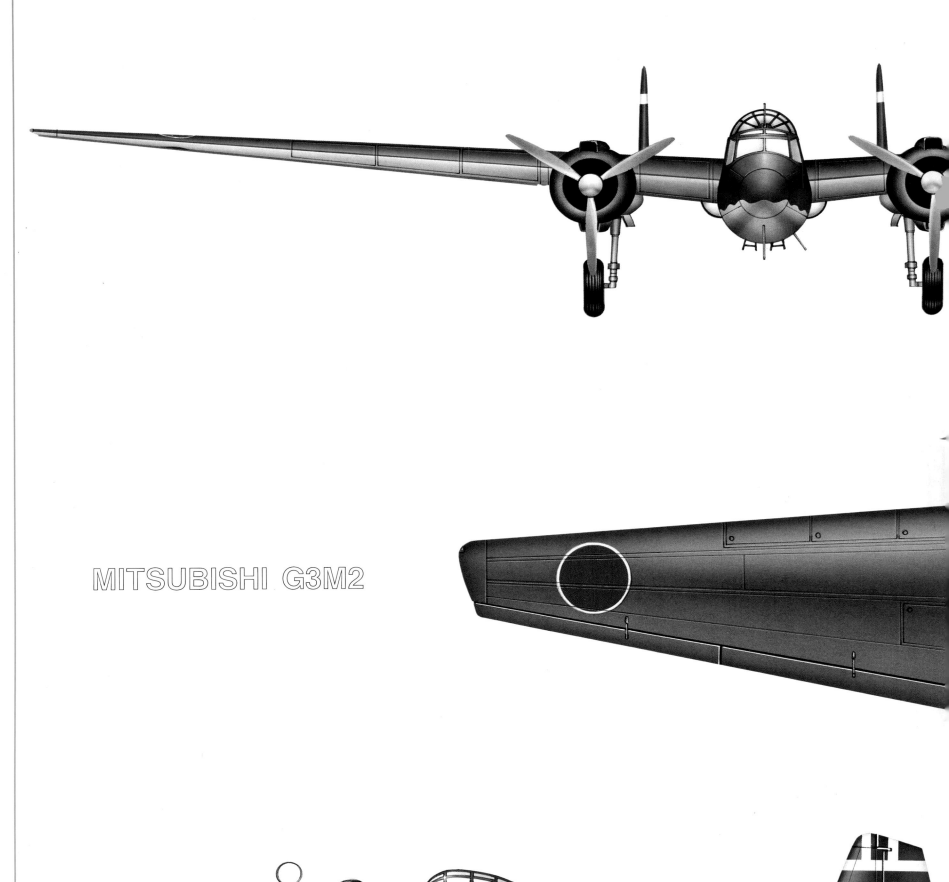

MITSUBISHI G3M2

R2-322

G3M2 of the Kisarazu Kokutai. The horizontal band on the rudder indicates the aircraft of a section leader.

In Japan, as in Germany, during the years of peace, ocean crossings or sporting events represented the most suitable and effective means of revealing to the world the enormous potential, achieved almost by surprise, of its aeronautical industry. In the years immediately prior to World War II, a series of intercontinental flights carried out by a modern twin-engine aircraft built by Mitsubishi caused a sensation. These included a round-the-world flight, sponsored by the daily newspaper *Mainichi Shimbun,* and carried out between August 26, and October 20, 1939, by an aircraft christened *Nippon* and registered J-BAC I: a total of more than 32,820 miles (52,850 km) were covered in 194 hours of flying time. This aircraft was a G3M2 model modified for civilian use and was the same as that which, little more than a year later, was to become famous for a feat of a very different kind: the sinking of the British battleships *Prince of Wales* and *Repulse* off Malaysia on December 10, 1941. During this operation (representing a second setback for the Allies after Pearl Harbor), the Mitsubishi bombers played a determining role, thanks mainly to their great range which made action possible in areas considered by the British and American high commands to be outside the range of the Japanese air force.

The G3M2 (designated NELL in the Allies' code, while the military transport model derived from it was known as TINA) constituted the main force in the Japanese navy's bomber units during the first year of the war, and a total of 1,048 were built up to 1943. The project had been launched in great secrecy in 1933, on the instigation of Admiral Isoroku Yamamoto, who was director of the technical division of the Aeronautical Office of the Imperial Navy at the time. Yamamoto, convinced of the need to build a long-range land plane capable of supporting the carrier-based aircraft in naval operations, succeeded in gaining approval for the program and for the immediate construction of a prototype.

This prototype (designed by Sueo Honjo, Tomio Kubo, and Nobuhiko Kusabake and designated Ka-9) made its maiden flight in April 1934 and immediately produced excellent results. The aircraft had been completed without taking military specifications into account, and, in June 1935, following a long series of evaluations, it was joined by the first of 21 prototypes built with a future military function in mind.

The initial G3M1 version went into production a year later. The bomber was an all-metal mid-wing monoplane, with retractable landing gear, characterized by double tail fins and powered by a pair of Mitsubishi Kinsei radial engines. Only 34 of this variant were built, and on their completion production continued with the principal G3M2 version. The latter (fitted with more powerful engines) was divided into two subseries (G3M2 Model 21 and G3M2 Model 22), of which 343 and approximately 400 aircraft were built respectively. The final variant (built exclusively by Nakajima from 1941), the G3M2 Model 23, was provided with 1,300 hp engines and larger fuel tanks, making it the fastest aircraft and the one with the greatest range.

The G3M made its operative debut in August 1937, during the second Sino-Japanese conflict. Following Japan's entry into the war, the Mitsubishi bombers took part in all operations in the Pacific islands, although they were gradually joined by the more modern G4Ms. The G3Ms were also used both as military and civilian transport planes. In the latter sector, the converting of 20 or so G3M2s in 1939 for commercial use should be mentioned. They were used mainly by the Nippon Koku K.K. and the Dai Nippon Koku K.K. airlines.

color plate
Mitsubishi G3M2 707th Naval Air Corps - Java 1942

Aircraft:	Mitsubishi G3M2
Nation:	Japan
Manufacturer:	Mitsubishi Jukogyo KK
Type:	Bomber
Year:	1937
Engine:	2 Mitsubishi Kinsei 41,14-cylinder radial, air-cooled, 1,075 hp each
Wingspan:	82 ft (25 m)
Length:	53 ft 11 in (16.45 m)
Height:	12 ft 1 in (3.68 m)
Weight:	17,637 lb (8,000 kg) loaded
Maximum speed:	232 mph (373 km/h) at 13,715 ft (4,180 m)
Ceiling:	29,950 ft (9,130 m)
Range:	2,722 miles (4,380 m)
Armament:	1 × 20 mm cannon; 4 machine guns; 1,764 lb (800 kg) of bombs
Crew:	7

Two Mitsubishi G3M's of the Mihoro Kokutai. The aircraft in the foreground is a G3M2, the other a G3M1. The differences in the dorsal defensive armament are clearly visible.

CONTENTS